ACRES IN THE

When the cab pulled up to Roxy's loft building . . .

Jonathan turned to her. 'If a woman doesn't invite me up for coffee at the end of a date, I feel lousy.'

She smiled. 'OK. Come up.'

She wound up making tea for them. They sipped it at the long harvest table.

It was funny, he thought. He was an attractive man with a clear sense of his own sexual power and he couldn't even begin to remember all the flight attendants and socialites and secretaries he'd slept with. But now he was really puzzled by just the right way to reach out and touch this beautiful woman whom he wanted more than anything in the world.

'Roxy,' he said, 'do you think we might have a future together?'

She seemed to mull it over for a moment. 'I suppose we should find out,' she said finally.

He caressed her hair, then her cheek.

'We're looking for trouble,' she murmured.

'No,' he said, as he kissed her neck, her hair.

'Big trouble . . .'

**Books in the HAROLD ROBBINS
PRESENTS™ Series and available from
New English Library:**

BLUE SKY by Sam Stewart
AT THE TOP by Michael Donoval
THE WHITE KNIGHT by Carl. F. Furst
HIGH STAKES by John Fischer

Acres in the Sky

Adrien Lloyd

NEW ENGLISH LIBRARY
Hodder and Stoughton

Copyright © 1986 by Pocket Books, a division of Simon and Schuster Inc.

First published in the United States of America by Pocket Books

NEL Paperback edition 1987

HAROLD ROBBINS PRESENTS is a trademark of Harold Robbins

Printed and bound in Great Britain for Hodder and Stoughton Paperbacks, a division of Hodder and Stoughton Ltd., Mill Road, Dunton Green, Sevenoaks, Kent TN13 2YA. (Editorial Office: 47 Bedford Square, London WC1B 3DP) by Richard Clay Ltd., Bungay, Suffolk.

British Library C.I.P.

Lloyd, Adrien

Acres in the sky: a novel.—
(Harold Robbins presents).
I.Title
813'.54[F]   PS3562.L61
ISBN 0-450-41735-2

HE HAD IT all in the palm of his hand.

Jonathan Broad looked out over the dais at the sea of famous faces, all come to pay homage to his talent, his vision, his daring. The Broad Palace had gone up over the sound and fury of a legion of tight-asses and old maids who had accused him of mauling the face of the city in order to remake it in his own image. Now it stood, at 53rd and Fifth, occupying a site that had been for half a century the province of three small Beaux-Arts town houses perfectly fine in their day but out of step with the pulse and the needs of the modern city. Now, in the late afternoon sunshine, the Palace shot up into the sky like a silver arrow, a sleek missile of a building that threatened at any moment to take flight. It was, Jonathan thought, the thing in the world of which he was most proud.

There was much to be proud of. At 35, he had made his name into a household word . . . or, to some, he realized, a household curse. He had taken a certain amount of wealth—admittedly, a great amount—and was on his way to turning that amount into something incalculable, unimaginable. He was transforming the Broad Company, started by his grandfather, Jan

Broot, the Dutch plasterer turned Bay Ridge landlord, into something else, something bigger: an empire. The Broad Company now had a hand in hotels—already they owned seven important hostelries in Manhattan and two in Atlantic City—as well as commercial and residential real estate. There was no ceiling for the Broad Company, nor, Jonathan felt with an assurance that seemed almost illicit, for himself.

"Ladies and gentlemen," announced Judd Belton, the silver-haired former New York Congressman who had found a second career as a toastmaster, "today is Broad Palace Day in our city!"

A wave of applause broke over the audience, which Jonathan acknowledged with a smile. The crowd glittered with the famous! Marisa Berenson and Marion Javits, socialites Nan Kempner and Amanda Burden and Cornelia Guest, Thomas Hoving, Jerry Zipkin, Barbara Walters and Merv Adelson, Bill Agee and Mary Cunningham, and more, many many more. The rich and the powerful and the famous, and they all wanted a part of him. Why? Because he bespoke money and power—their language too—and the members of this particular club stuck together. As he thought about this, Jonathan thought too about the ancestors of these fine folk turning their backs on Jan Broot, with his plaster dust and mutton chops and thick chowderhead accent. But that was history, and this was a day for the pleasures of the present.

There were more speeches and testimonials and then it was time to cut the tape. In the company of architect Wilson Marriner, Jonathan Broad did the honors. Another wave of applause broke out. Jonathan cast a glance at his father, David, beaming with pride, and his sister Merry, waving to him. Just to the

right of his father was Stella. Jonathan looked at his
wife, dressed in her best—and her best was better
than anyone's—and she gave him a smile back, the
coldness of which only he could detect.

"Ladies and gentlemen," Jonathan began—he
wasn't much for public speaking but it was a role that
had been thrust on him and he was the sort who made
a point of tackling and overcoming the things that he
didn't feel comfortable with—"it is a proud moment
for me to be standing here, before the beautiful
building which bears my family's name, and to know
that we have given New York City a small return on all
that it's given us."

More applause. It wasn't so hard, Jonathan
thought. Making speeches was only really difficult
when you were asking for something.

Jonathan went through the nods to the architect
and the mayor and everyone else he was obliged to
mention. "But I don't want to keep you too long," he
allowed. "There is so much for you to see—please, be
my guests, and see the Broad Palace. It is waiting for
you."

Again the applause and he stepped out into the
crowd and it was splendid. As the guests filed into the
astonishing atrium, fifteen stories high, complete with
waterfall, stands of bamboo, and thousands of bro-
meliads and orchids, the string quartet that Stella had
gotten in from Juilliard broke into a medieval air.
Young men—most of them hand-picked by Stella for
their handsome faces and well-made bodies—were
dressed in brightly colored leather jerkins, like medieval pages, their strong legs clad in green tights, tucked
into boots. Some of them carried lutes, others carried
trays of food. It was lavish and a little ridiculous and

terrific, Jonathan thought. Stella certainly had a sense of show business. But then that was, after all, her alleged background. She had wanted to be an actress. No—she had wanted to be a star. She *was* an actress —indeed, she never, even for a moment, stopped being an actress.

"Fabulous job, Jonathan," came a voice from behind. He turned; it was Evangeline Gouletas Carey, who knew a thing or two about real estate. He kissed her, thanked her, moved along. Next came Felicia Moss, an oil heiress with the best ass in town, one he had been able to sample a few years ago in Acapulco. They kissed—one definitely more lingering than Mrs. Carey's peck on the cheek—and he moved on. Out of the corner of his eye he could see Stella working her part of the room. She, too, had a kiss for everyone— what would AIDS do to the kissy-kiss world of New York high society?—and he noticed too the eyes of all the men, and most of the women, trained on his beautiful wife. For she *was* beautiful, amazingly beautiful. Racehorses, skyscrapers, and a certain species of beautiful women share the same kind of fine lines, and Stella certainly had them. Tall, beautifully proportioned, full-breasted and long-limbed, with a startling mane of blue black hair worn wild and devastatingly sexy, ice blue eyes that promised everything and revealed nothing, and the smoothest copper-colored skin of the sort that everyone who went south to the sun risked cancer for but never managed to get, and a way of carrying herself that connoted both grace and risk. She was a rare one, Stella was; when they made her they broke the mold. He only wished the mold had been broken sooner.

From behind him he heard a sudden piercing

shriek. He whirled around and came face to face with a magnificent peacock in full courtship display. The glorious bird, with its iridescent plumage, happened to have been saddled with one of the worst voices in the animal kingdom, but with that fan of feathers, who cared? Again, Stella's showmanship paid off. Some might have found it all vulgar and ostentatious —but those people weren't invited tonight. Tonight was the night for people who, like the peacock, liked to display themselves.

"Prince Jonathan," called a voice in heavy, Borscht Belt Yiddish accent. He turned again—this time away from Phillipe de Montebello, Director of the Metropolitan Museum, and Mrs. Vincent Astor, New York's leading philanthropist, and was confronted with Jaysie Gartner, a popular comedian who had a regular berth at the Broad Casino in Atlantic City and was known nationally for his occasional substitute hosting of the Tonight Show. Gartner was dressed up as a court jester, except for his Reebok sneakers. "Such a building you built, *tattela,*" Gartner shrieked. "Tell me, you got indoor plumbing here?"

Those in the immediate area chuckled; Jonathan waved and moved on through the crowd. Jaysie Gartner was OK in Atlantic City—wasn't doing anybody any harm—but Jonathan was pretty sure he had told Stella to leave him out of the festivities. Now he saw her glancing at him, and smiling her private smile, the bitch. He crossed the atrium to be at her side.

"Problem, dear?" she said under her breath as she nodded and whispered sweet nothings to passersby.

"What's that clown Jaysie Gartner doing here in that stupid outfit?" he demanded in a whisper. "I told you I didn't want him here."

"Darling, don't be a stiff. A little comic relief never hurt. Anyway, how could we not include Jaysie? He's like a member of the family."

"Your family, maybe," he said, wanting to hurt her, "whoever that is."

She turned to stare at him. He didn't know why he still wanted to make love to her, but when she looked at him this way he found himself responding so naturally and uncontrollably. "Shove it, Jonathan," she said coolly, and walked off, shaking her ass to torment him.

His sister Merry hustled over. "What's she up to now?" Merry whispered to her brother.

"Oh, Merry, please," said Jonathan wearily. He loved his sister dearly, but he didn't need her to point out Stella's all too obvious bad points.

"I just won't stand for her making you miserable, Jonathan," Merry said grimly. "Not tonight, not on your night."

He leaned over to give her a hug. "Don't worry, kiddo," he said. "As long as us Broads stick together, no one can hurt us."

He was kidding . . . but not really. They hugged each other and then there was Papa David, breaking away from a group of bankers to be with his children. "Look at this picture," David said. "My two jewels."

They both hugged their father. Why not? He was a huggable man, to them anyway. To the rest of the world, David Broad seemed an aloof, unreadable sort of man. All his life he had proved himself gifted at making money, at steering things along, at management, at grooming his son for the succession. But what the world did not see was the endless resources of love beneath the worldly, temporal concerns. Papa

David was a wonderful father. No one knew David's playfulness, his tenderness, his warmth, except Merry and Jonathan. Now Jonathan stared at his father. He hadn't looked well for weeks. "Are you all right, Papa?" he asked.

"Am I all right?" responded the elder Broad. "How could I be less than wonderful on the night that the Broad Palace opens to the public? Your mother would have been so proud of you two," he said to his children. "Her daughter Merry, for all the beautiful designs you've brought to this enterprise, and her son Jonathan for having the vision to get this project off the ground."

The mayor of New York City, the Honorable Edward Koch, politician and character *extraordinaire,* sauntered over to them. "David, your *kvelling"*— Yiddish for being proud—"is lighting up the room and this is one big room to light up."

David and Koch enjoyed a laugh together. But then, without warning, Jaysie Gartner was back. "Look who's here," said Jaysie, in his idiotic court jester's uniform, shaking his sleigh bells, "our friend the mayor. Greetings, Ed."

"Greetings, Jaysie."

"Some playground, huh?" Jaysie marveled, looking around. "And Jonathan here only had to kill five or six people to get his way."

There was a sudden pall. Jonathan gave Jaysie a hard stare. He was coked out of his head. "Pull yourself together, Jaysie," Jonathan warned.

"Come, Jaysie," said Merry brightly, linking her arm in the comedian's. "You and I are going to tour around."

Jaysie gave a Groucho-like leer, tapped an imaginary cigar, and said, "I'd like to tour around in your hills and valleys, lady."

That was it. Jonathan excused himself, signaled his bodyguards, and, in a moment, two young men built like oxen discreetly escorted the hapless Jaysie Gartner into one of the fleet of waiting cars that Jonathan always kept on hand. Tomorrow, Jaysie's contract with the Broad Casino would be bought out.

Merry, shaken, took Jonathan by the arm and led him to the bridge over the moat that ran through the atrium. Atop the moat, Jonathan surrendered himself to the photographers' flashbulbs. Tomorrow his face would be everywhere—WWD, page six of the *Post,* the *Voice.* It was a handsome face, he himself realized. In that respect, too, he had been blessed. He favored not the stout, pasty look of the Dutch Broots, but rather his mother's people, the Fourgets of Paris. His mother, Genevieve, dead ten years now, was the perfect antidote to his father's own phlegmatic personality, very French, not so much pretty as stylish, with that great sense of personal style that certain French women have. Twice a year she flew to Paris to visit family and, perhaps more importantly, to case the couture houses. She came from a long line of *parfumiers* who made fortunes and then lost it all at Deauville and made it back during the war in the black market and then lost it with a postwar generation of alcoholics and malcontents and black sheep. Like the Fourgets, Jonathan possessed chiseled features and deep-set, clear blue eyes. Like the Fourgets, he had a lean physique, hearkening back to some distant French swashbuckling ancestors rather than those stolid Dutch burghers. And, like the Fourget men, he had turned prematurely gray in his twenties, so that now he had a shock of silver hair that was uniquely incongruous with his youthful appearance.

His physical presence, Jonathan realized, was just one more piece of effective ammunition in the arsenal with which he confronted the world. Not that he confronted the world with any sense of anguish or fury. No, he had a good enough time at it, seeing himself as a sort of soldier of fortune. Success, fame, power, and glory—these were all games, the best sort of games in the world. Games that were so much fun that they made the games of youth—the ringelevio and mumbletypeg and dodgeball—pale utterly in comparison.

It was this sense of gamesmanship that had attracted him to Stella in the first place. When he first encountered her, she had been a reservations clerk at Le Printemps, his hotel at Lexington and 63rd. He took one look—one lingering look—at Stella and knew she was all wrong for Le Printemps. She was no dewy vision of springtime; she was sultry summer heat. Le Printemps, a demure refuge for ladies in from Connecticut on shopping trips, was no place for somebody who looked like Stella Nevins.

He had her transferred to Montague's, the newest Broad Hotel, on West 57th Street. Jonathan had hired Dewey Mizoguchi, a screaming Eurasian queen with the highest cheekbones in New York City and the most flamboyant—but somehow "right"—taste of this last quarter of the twentieth century, to do the joint top to bottom, and Dewey had outdone himself. Purple became the color of the hotel—purple in all its shades, wine and lavender and aubergine and plum, and then things like tamarind and pinot noir, which Dewey would show him in swatches and paint chips over spare Japanese lunches of odd-smelling fish. The place took off like a rocket, and Stella, Jonathan realized after that first look at her, would be a perfect addition. They had her dress in violet leather and burgundy suede with purple ribbons through her waist-length black hair and brooches and bracelets of amethysts as big as purple onions. It wasn't long before everyone knew who was the reservations clerk at Montague's and her picture was featured first in WWD and then in spreads in *Vogue* and *Bazaar*.

But Stella had bigger things planned than modeling purple leather Claude Montana jackets for Conde Nast publications. She went after Jonathan like a Royal Canadian Mountie—the kind of Mountie who always got her man. At the time, he was involved— fairly heavily—with Abigail Forester, who had a perch on the Landmarks Preservation Commission and who had stared at him across a walnut conference table as if she were Joan of Arc and he were Attila the Hun.

When he first met her, Jonathan had taken Abigail for a perfect Park Avenue ice maiden. A Grace Kelly look-alike, somewhere in her early to mid-forties (it was hard to tell with rich women, who had cosmetic surgery so available to them), she had the whitest porcelain skin, the shiniest blue eyes, and the most golden hair he had ever seen, massed around her head in a scrupulously coiffed French twist. It didn't take long for him to get the message that she could be thawed. The first time she took down her hair for him, and he saw the shower of gold that reached her waist in her blue chintz bedroom with the four-poster canopied bed, he threatened to come before the first act.

It was good with Abigail. And it was good with the occasional flight attendant, and the horny socialites after the charity balls, and the dark-skinned chambermaids in the linen closets of his hotels. He was getting all he needed, and the idea of an involved, continuing relationship—a commitment—was as welcome as a case of shingles. And then along came Stella. She was smart, Stella was. When it came to the particular kind of smarts that ensured getting what you wanted, Stella left him in the dust.

"Smile, Jonathan," Merry whispered.

He turned to the photographers. The flashbulbs kept going off. He remembered to smile, until he caught a glimpse of his wife staring at him, her own secret smile on her lips. If it weren't for Stella, life would be very good for him. It wasn't fair, he thought, forcing himself to smile once again as the bursts of light from the cameras blinded him.

"Ladies and gentlemen," said Peter Duchin, the famous society bandleader, "Mr. and Mrs. Jonathan Broad invite you to join them as they dance."

Duchin's orchestra broke into the strains of "Cheek to Cheek." Jonathan had wanted something elegant and classy, and certainly nothing could be so more than music associated with Rogers and Astaire. But the lyrics, exalting heaven in the arms of one's partner, were ironic, even bitter, in light of this first dance he was dancing with his wife for the benefit of his guests, most of whom probably suspected the discord that had entered into their marriage.

"What a delightful choice for a first dance, Jonathan," said Stella, "tripping the light fantastic" as Liz Smith would no doubt report tomorrow in the *News*.

11

"Our song," he said sarcastically, spinning her out and then back. They danced perfectly together. It wasn't surprising. Jonathan did most things perfectly —or at least outstandingly well. He had a five handicap in golf; his tennis game had once afforded him national ranking in the juniors; he had made crew at Princeton.

"So here you are," she said through the tight lips that formed enough of a smile—or so she thought—to fool the cameras. "Mr. Whiz Kid. The Master Builder. Dancing with his beautiful wife."

"Why don't you leave it alone?" he said. "You're the great actress, aren't you? Came to New York to see your name in lights, right up there next to Helen Hayes. So what if you got stuck on the casting couch—you're still a great actress. So here's your golden opportunity, Stella—*act*. Go ahead, be the perfect little wife. Act your goddamn heart out."

She looked at him as though she'd like to drive a knife through his heart. And the thing was that he could imagine it. He could imagine her destroying anything or anyone that got in her way.

"Hi, Ann," Stella cried, with a wave for Ann Getty, wife of Gordon Getty, son of the billionaire J.P. Getty. Jonathan noted the brilliance of Stella's smile, so incandescent for the rich and the powerful, for anyone who could advance her in some way. That was the way her smile had been for him that fateful day long past in the discreet, teal blue and mustard lobby of Le Printemps. She had been wearing a beige jersey dress and her hair was in a bun. There were reading glasses perched on the end of her nose. Madame Librarian. Except that when she saw him, she looked up and gave him her smile and stretched like a big, beautiful cat, and he watched her breasts move beneath the jersey and wondered what they would be like, and she saw him wondering, and it wasn't more than a few hours later that she was showing him some files and bending over him and pushing her tits against his shoulder.

That sort of thing happened all the time. People were always pressing against him, always wanting to get the feel of him, and sometimes he pressed back. But with Stella, he was caught unaware. Her sheer sensual magnetism was overwhelming, intoxicating. He asked her, that very day, to join him for dinner. She stared at him—she didn't pretend to be demure; she didn't ask to be joined by her aunt or her mother or her sister. What shall I wear? she asked. Something suitable for dancing, he suggested.

They went down to Area that night, then one of New York's newest clubs. She wore something suitable for dancing all right—a sheer pink wrapping, with buttons shaped like peppermint sticks. Unwrap me for Christmas, every cell of her body screamed out. And later that night, when they went to bed—and again there was no coyness, only a certain kind of eagerness, a certain kind of avidity that he found unbelievably exciting—she showed him things he'd never experienced before despite all the women he'd been with.

"Only you could get a hard-on at a time like this," Stella smirked, as they danced close together. "I'm flattered."

The music ended; there was applause.

"You bitch," he hissed. She looked back at him with a cold, glittering eye.

"Jonathan," gushed a voice from behind. He

13

whirled around. It was Lolly Hunnicutt, one of Abigail Forester's closest friends. "Congratulations, you've left Mr. Trump in the dust, Jonathan dear," she said, offering him her cheek. He kissed it dutifully, and she moved on.

"A fan?" Stella asked, her eyebrow arched.

Soon it was time to sit down for dinner. The affair was being handled by Great Moments, New York's most prominent catering service, which had picked up on the medieval theme of the Palace and had prepared an opulent six-course feast, including leek soup, partridge, wild field lettuce salad, and, for dessert, a devastating wassail mousse. Throughout the dinner the Juilliard group kept up a lilting background of medieval airs, and young men circulated from table to table with juggling exhibitions, minstrel recitations, and other delightful excesses.

Jonathan circulated from table to table, unable to eat for the excitement of it all.

"Splendid, Jonathan," said Philip Johnson, dean of American architects. "Absolutely splendid."

"You've brought a sense of drama back to New York that it's sorely missed," said publisher Rupert Murdoch, who would surely run much coverage of the event tomorrow in his *Post* and *Village Voice*.

"This young man is a showman nonpareil," announced the empress of style, New York's premier tastemaker, Diana Vreeland. "We haven't seen his like since P.T. Barnum."

Jonathan kissed the hand of Mrs. Vreeland, encrusted as it was with precious jewels. "You're very kind," he said.

More speeches, more dancing, more beautiful

women coming to embrace him, more men looking at him with admiration and envy. Jonathan stared up at the roof of the atrium, with its canopy of orchids, its flight of exotic birds. He had made this. *He had made it by the force of his own will.* Nobody could take that away from him. Not Stella, not anyone.

At three in the morning the party was over and it was time for the *paparazzi* to attack in earnest. Stella Nevins Broad ducked into the ladies room to make sure everything was in place. She looked into the bronze-tinted mirror and liked what she saw. Stella knew that one of her strong points was her ability to take an inventory of herself and to see to it that everything was in tiptop condition. And, she noted as she examined herself, it was. Hair: perfect. Make-up: perfect. She peered at the hand-painted, sapphire silk Caroline Hererra dress that had cost $17,500 and saw a speck of a smudge at the yoke. She wet a tissue and dabbed at it. Smudge gone. Clothes perfect.

Thank God for good bones, she thought, as she took another moment to look at herself. It was one thing she got from her father—the only thing she had gotten from her father. From photographs of him, she had seen a craggy, rangy man of the West. He had disappeared when she was four, but he left her with that same kind of rangy frame that never showed fat nor age. From her mother she had gotten nothing to speak of. Dot Nevins—now there was a name, one that perfectly expressed the essence of the woman. A dot. A flyspeck of humanity. She grew up feeling repulsed by her mother. She was a practical nurse, and her legs were too big and full of varicose veins; she wore

15

heavy-duty hose, and when she got home at night she sat in her ratty old armchair and rolled the hose down below her knees and drank a Schlitz. Watched "The Lucy Show" or "Andy Griffith," then fell asleep in her chair, and Stella would have to wake her and she'd be snoring to break the bank and Stella would want to be away, so far away, where things were beautiful and shiny and didn't smell of moth balls and old ice blue Secret and the inevitable scent of sweat.

She lived at home until she was seventeen. Mama, brother McCoy, and Stella, the perfect family unit. Did she mention that brother McCoy liked to set fires and run an occasional second-story job? Stella kept plugging away, did her best in school, even if her best meant thrusting her well-formed tits at the instructors so they'd remember her and give her a good grade. She might have hung in there, graduated high school and settled down with some muscular and humpy boob if Adolph hadn't moved in with them.

Adolph was Dot's second husband. He was a fore-man down at the bottling plant, and he was built like a Mack truck. As soon as he had moved in—when she was fourteen—he kept an eye on her. And then, when Stella was sixteen and her mother had to go into the hospital to do something about her damned varicose veins Adolph jumped her. Well, not exactly jumped her, but crept into her bed.

He smelled of hops, she thought. And he was so big. His hands were like hams, his shoulders were like boulders, and his cock was like a great long lance grinding into her.

—You're beautiful, Stella, you're beautiful.

It happened more than once. She even got to like it

16

a little, she had to admit. But she decided that if she were beautiful—if she were the kind of woman that men wanted—then she'd make them pay for it. A bus, a suitcase, and New York followed . . . and lots of men, until she found what she was looking for.

The door to the powder room opened and Stella watched Merry Broad enter. Merry stopped for a moment when she realized with whom she was sharing the facility.

"Oh, it's you," Merry said.

Stella said nothing, taking a gold-handled brush from her bag and running it through her mane of hair. Jonathan's sister was a wimp—a rich little wimp, but a wimp nonetheless. People went on and on about her skills as an interior designer and maybe they were right, but she was thirty-two years old, nothing special to look at, and didn't have a steady man in her life.

"You shouldn't have tinted the mirrors bronze, Merry," Stella said, as she langorously brushed her hair. "People are going to think they have liver damage."

"Thanks for the feedback, Stella."

Stella threw the brush into her bag and clicked it closed, turning to face her sister-in-law. "You're up past your bedtime, aren't you, dear?"

"My bedtime isn't your business," Merry snapped back.

"Seems your bedtime isn't anybody's business," Stella returned.

"When are you going to get out of our lives, Stella?" Merry demanded. "None of us can stand you. It isn't a secret anymore. Thank God Jonathan's caught on to you."

"When I'm ready, gumdrop," said Stella with a fierce smile. "And don't worry, I won't make any trouble for anyone."

"You're an animal!"

"Hiss!" Stella exploded into her sister-in-law's startled face, and when she saw the shock there, she laughed and pushed open the brass door and went out into the lightning storm of flashbulbs and the shouts of the *paparazzi*.

"Stella! Stella! Stella!"

It was a chant, and she opened her mouth wide and showed her gleaming white teeth and smiled for them. She made good copy and they loved her and she let them shoot her. Why not? Seeing her picture in the papers still gave her a thrill, and maybe Dot was back home putting together a scrapbook.

"Give it to us, Stella!" they shouted, and she postured for them, and dragged her $200,000 sable wrap on the floor, and showed some leg, and if it had been worth her while she would have shown some bare titty too. But she wasn't giving anything away, not anything.

"Hey, Stella baby! Little Stella Nevins!" Something stopped her in her tracks—an animal awareness of something wrong, something dangerous. She looked through the screen of exploding flashbulbs until she found a face that was familiar to her. There. The fat one with the greasy hair and the patchy beard.

She felt a sudden downward lurch in her stomach, as if she were on an elevator that had broken loose from its cable.

"Stella, baby!" the voice—the face—repeated with a leer as he fired off flashbulbs.

It was Jerry Castriata. Fat Jerry.

She pulled up her wrap from where it was dangling on the floor and put it over her shoulders, bringing it up around her face, hiding her face in it. She pushed through the *paparazzi,* headed for the waiting limo.

"Hey, Stella baby! Don't be a stranger!" he called.

She didn't look back, but she could hear him laughing. Her heart beating furiously, she pressed on, seeking escape.

2

JONATHAN SAT IN his aerie at the top of the Broad Palace and looked out at the city while Wilson Marriner complained about the construction company they were using at the new Silver Lode Casino in Atlantic City.

His architect complained too much, Jonathan thought, continuing to gaze out at the city. He loved being this high up. The idea of consolidating his living and office quarters on the fifty-eighth floor of the Broad Palace had been an inspired one. Here he had a seventeen-room apartment spread out over three floors: a floor of office space; a gymnasium and swimming pool; a greenhouse and a meditation garden. The open-market cost of all this was, of course, almost incalculable, but the last of the remaining turret apartments had just been sold to Windy Merchant, a 29-year-old filmmaker with the third-highest grossing film of all time, for the ripe sum of $17 million dollars.

"OK, Wilson," he said abruptly, cutting off his architect's dirge, "I'll get on it."

He picked up another line; his secretary, Lotte, was a master at stacking calls, one of just a few reasons why he paid her $45,000 a year, excluding benefits. "Mike? How're you doing, buddy?" he said expansively. It was Mike Mulligan, a *Daily News* columnist who wrote such favorable pieces about all the things Jonathan Broad did for this city that many people accused him of being a tout. "Listen, kid, I'm flying down to Atlantic City tonight. Wanna come? Do a piece on me as 'the master Monopoly player as seen on Ventnor Avenue?'"

Jonathan smiled broadly as Mike Mulligan lapped it up like clotted cream. Maybe he really was a tout: "OK, babe. I'll have the car pick you up at 6:22. See you then."

He clicked onto the intercom. "A Miss Lolly Hunnicutt on 32, Jonathan," said Lotte, who had a delivery like the late, great Thelma Ritter.

He picked up. "Lolly?" he said, to Abigail Forester's great friend.

"Jonathan," came back the French vanilla voice. "It was so lovely last night. I just wanted to let you know."

This one was cut from the same cloth as Abigail, but a few years younger. Like Abigail she had perfect blond hair, a nose so sculptured you could use it as the paradigm of all noses, and eyes of Newport Sound blue. "How nice of you to call, Lolly."

"It's been so long since I've seen you and Stella, Jonathan . . ."

"Stella and I have been pretty much on our own schedules these days, Lolly. Together we kind of cover the waterfront."

There was a pause. "Well, can I extend some hospitality to you individually, Jonathan?" she said discreetly. "Dinner some night?"

21

He looked out at the city and smiled. These society matrons had hot pants, no doubt about it. But then look at Lolly's husband—Oscar Hunnicutt, pushing seventy-five, with about $100 million behind him, along with two or three prostate operations. The lady needed stud service, and it was either him, the chauffeur, or the Mexican gardener. What did it matter that he was the sometime interest of her best friend? Abigail must have told her he passed muster in the sack department and here she was, bold as brass.

"That sounds terrific, Lolly," he lied, having no plans to enmesh himself in that particular trap. "Why don't I give you a call when I get back from Europe?" Delicious valedictions followed and then he rose from his desk and did fifty push-ups. He didn't want to let anything go; he was, after all, only thirty-five years old.

Lotte entered as he was on his forty-third push-up. "You're gonna get sweat stains on your custom-made shirt," she warned in her foghorn voice.

"Don't . . . 44 . . . worry . . . 45 . . . about my . . . 46 . . . damned Turnbull . . . 47 . . . and Asser . . . 48 . . . shirt . . . 49 . . . 50."

He lay on the floor for a moment, panting.

"At $200 a shirt, I can worry. Listen, Jonathan," she said, sitting on the edge of his vast onyx desk, "when I was growing up $200 wasn't a shirt. $200 was a down payment."

He laughed. "Never."

"Never? Ask your father."

He jumped up and did a few limbering exercises. "Get me a grapefruit juice, will you, Lotte?"

She went to the fridge and took out a few grapefruits, which she cut up and squeezed in the Braun

22

citrus juicer. Jonathan only liked juice when it was fresh . . . and why shouldn't he have what he wanted?

Lotte was one of life's definite prizes, he thought as he sipped from the glass. With her astringent personality and sardonic humor, she effectively took the wind out of his sails and kept him moored in reality.

It was 11:30 and he had been going since 5:00. He always woke at five, worked in his apartment until six, got to his desk at 6:30. (Lotte refused to join him there until 7:00.) Today, he had already had three meetings: one with Sidney Farrell and Anderson Kendall, his two main hands, one with a consortium of Japanese investors, and one with a reporter from *Time* magazine.

"Don't work out too hard," Lotte called from her desk, where she was enjoying her mid-morning cigarette, a habit he deplored but could not break her of.

In the gymnasium, his trainer, Pablo Quitta, was waiting for him. Pablo was a man of 45 and if Jonathan could look like him at that age, he would be more than happy.

"Hola, Señor Broad," called Pablo.

Jonathan had tried to get Pablo to call him by his name, but Pablo's inbred Latin sense of decorum and social stratification had made that impossible.

"Hola, Pablo." Jonathan suited up and for the next hour Pablo led him through a series of demanding exercises. After that it was forty laps in the pool and some diving, and then a rubdown from Pablo. "You have the body of a much younger man, Señor Broad," said Pablo.

Jonathan closed his eyes and submitted to Pablo's strong and disciplined touch. Without the ministrations of Pablo—and of Abigail Forester—he would be knotted from head to toe. "In that respect, you are lucky, Señor Broad," Pablo said, kneading his shoulders. "In many respects, you are lucky."

After his shower and sauna, it was 1:15, and Jonathan walked the short distance over to Doubles, the exclusive private club in the Sherry-Netherland where he would be lunching today with his father.

The maitre d' greeted him with his usual deference, bordering on obsequiousness. "Good afternoon, Leon," Jonathan said, striding to his usual table where his father was already seated. En route, Jonathan waved to a few of his friends: Leona Helmsley, of Helmsley Hotels; Geraldine Stutz, president of Bendel's; and Felix Rohatyn, the investment banker.

"I'm not late for you, Dad, am I?" Jonathan said, as he sat down.

"No, no. Don't worry about it, Johnny. Let me look at you," said David Broad. "You're glowing."

"I just came from my workout and swim," he explained.

David shook his head. "How I admire your energy, son. When I was your age, I was already a middle-aged man. I had you and your sister to support and no time to play."

Jonathan took this, rightly, as a backhanded compliment. "It's not play, Dad. It's a way for me to stay on top of things. If I didn't treat my body right, I wouldn't last a week at this pace."

"Of course, Johnny," said David, sipping at his Dubonnet.

Jonathan ordered an Absolut with a twist. He allowed himself one hard drink a day—also medicinal, he told himself. Anyway, Dubonnet, which Jonathan's mother introduced to his father, would hardly

24

do the trick. But why was he justifying himself this way? At thirty-five years, his picture had been on the cover of *Fortune, The New York Times Magazine, Newsweek, Business Week,* and *Forbes,* so why was he sitting here justifying his daily routine to his father?

"It was a lovely party last night, Johnny," David said. "Stella outdid herself."

Jonathan nodded. "She can be a very talented woman," he allowed.

David watched him—and Jonathan was aware of David watching him—as the waiter brought over the Absolut and as Jonathan took a long swig. "It looks like you needed that," David said.

Jonathan shrugged. "What if I did?"

"I don't like it, Johnny. You seem to be under enormous strain and you're not telling me what it is . . ."

At this, Jonathan looked away and nodded at some other acquaintances. "Hi, Diane," he said, with a smile and a wave to *60 Minutes* correspondent Diane Sawyer.

"Look at me, Johnny," his father said sternly. "I don't like having lunch with you when you're carrying on like some sort of social butterfly."

Jonathan turned to look at his father. Usually the most benign of gentlemen, today he was being cranky and critical. His father generally treated Jonathan like a gift from God, and on close scrutiny he thought his color was off and he seemed to have a bit of a tremor in his hands. "You're not yourself, Dad," Jonathan said. "Are you feeling all right?"

"Of course I'm feeling all right," David said defensively. "It's only that I'm concerned about you . . ."

"Dad, you look thin. Have you been for a check-up lately?" Jonathan said solicitously.

"Oh, Jonathan, please. You're very smart and very agile but we are talking about *you.*" There was a silence. The waiter came with David's consommé royale and Jonathan's six blue points.

"You shouldn't be eating oysters, Johnny," his father said softly, with more tenderness. "So much hepatitis in raw shellfish, you know."

Jonathan sighed. His father was a good man, but he was a worrier. That was why he had not really managed to turn the legacy left him by his father, Jonathan's grandfather, into something grand, something fabulous. He was too conservative, too meek, too measured. Everyone in the financial community trusted his sense and his honesty, but he was not an empire-builder.

"Have you spoken to Merry today?" David asked.

"No," said Jonathan, swallowing an oyster.

"You should, you know. You should speak to your sister every day. When I'm gone, she's going to be alone in the world. The only person she'll have is you."

Jonathan put down his fork. "Hey, this is really a fun lunch, Dad. Real upbeat. Did you call me out today to put the fear of God in me and to tell me what a rotten brother and son I am?"

"Jonathan," said David, taken aback. "I was only suggesting that you and Merry . . ."

"Please, Dad. Merry's a big girl. I'm a big boy. We have a very good brother-sister relationship but we have our own lives to lead. And you have your own life to live," Jonathan added emphatically.

David stared at him with bloodshot, tired eyes.

"I'm only concerned for my children, Jonathan. When you have children—*if* you have children—you'll know what that feels like."

Jonathan sighed. "Let's change the subject, Dad. Listen, tonight I'm flying down to Atlantic City with Wilson Marriner and Mike Mulligan from the *News* . . ."

"Watch what you say, Johnny," David cautioned. "Mike seems like your friend, but friends are friends and family is family. Don't go shooting your mouth off about everything . . ."

What a mood he was in today, thought Jonathan, who girded himself and forged ahead. "Tomorrow, more meetings on River Park. I wondered if you wanted to join us for the meeting in the afternoon with Dennis Ogilvy?"

"Ogilvy? The city planner?"

"One and the same," said Jonathan. Ogilvy was responsible for waterfront restorations throughout the Eastern seaboard. His company had almost single-handedly rescued the inner cities of any number of decaying metropolises. Jonathan figured that he'd be a good collaborator on this, River Park, the grand New York Harbor restoration that Jonathan envisioned stretching from Hell's Kitchen all the way up to the 79th Street Boat Basin.

"I don't like the whole project." David sniffed, as if the project was in some way decayed.

"You never have," said Jonathan irritably.

"I've never understood why you wanted to open up that messy kettle of fish . . ."

"New York has the greatest harbor in the world," Jonathan said, stabbing the last of his blue point oysters and swallowing it whole, "and most New

27

Yorkers have absolutely no sense of it. In every other city where a harbor features prominently—San Francisco, Hong Kong, Singapore—you can feel the water, you can walk along it, you can eat crabs along it, and you can be a part of it. But not in New York."

"You're a little late, Jonathan. We've already got the South Street Seaport."

"It's not enough, Dad. It's quaint, but it's too small, it's too Disney World. With River Park, I'm talking about a major construction project that will open up this city."

"Jonathan, do you remember how Eisenhower always warned never to get involved in Southeast Asia? That it was a morass you could never get out of? Well, I give you the same sort of advice. *Stay out of the waterfront.*"

"You're wrong, Dad . . ."

"Look at Westway!" David said heatedly. "Look at the time and effort that went down the tubes there! Is that what you want?"

There was a silence as the waiter came to collect their plates and fill water glasses. When he left, they resumed the argument. "Listen, Dad," Jonathan said, "I can do it. I can take those rotting, crumbling old piers and I can turn them into pavilions that will be among the most spectacular public places of this century."

David stared at his son and then, with a grin, he shook his head. "I can't help believing you, Johnny. My Lord, when they passed out the confidence, you were certainly at the top of the line. In that respect, you are your mother's son. She could have a duchess or a prince eating out of her hand."

Jonathan saw his father take on that faraway aspect

that he had always had when he talked about Jonathan's late mother. His father had never found another woman to interest him the way Jonathan's mother had. That kind of romantic love seemed so far away from Jonathan's experience. What Stella had offered, in the beginning, was a rare kind of excitement, something better than ecstasy, but love? No, he thought not.

"Still," said David more soberly, as he picked at his lemon sole, "I can offer you no enthusiasm. It seems to me like the kind of grandstanding that can only lead to trouble. Besides that, your expectations of penetrating the waterfront without getting your hands seriously soiled strikes me as naïve."

"I've managed to do just that in Atlantic City," Jonathan said, stung.

"Indeed," said David. "But you can't always be the lucky one, Jonathan. Your life isn't one big hat trick. Take my advice and steer clear of it."

Jonathan stared at his father, then glanced down at his salad. He was a good man, but he lacked vision. For that reason, Jonathan had to take everything he said with a grain of salt.

"I'm getting to be an old man now, Jonathan," David said wearily.

"Oh, Dad. Don't start with . . ."

David held up a hand. "I'm getting to be an old man," he went on. "I look back on my life, Johnny, and everything falls into perspective. I've had a good life. I've had my disappointments, God knows, but I've been a lucky man. And the thing that made my life good is that I have had people I love in my life. Your mother, your sister, you." He leaned toward his son and gripped his forearm with his old, spotted

29

hand. "Don't go building empires, Jonathan, for the sake of avoiding the rest of your life. Don't lose sight of the trees for the forest, my boy."

"What are you saying, Dad?" Jonathan said hollowly.

"Make a life for yourself, Johnny. All this—" he said, indicating the plush room filled with the immaculately groomed, the rich, and the powerful--"all this counts for something, but not everything. Make a life with someone you love, have children, do what you were put on this earth to do."

"Make you a grandfather?" Jonathan said with a wry smile, trying to make a joke of it all.

"Do what you need to do, Johnny," David said unsmilingly, with great intensity. "Make a good life for yourself, my son. Nobody else can do it for you."

The racing-car-green convertible Bentley, circa 1947, pulled up in front of the elegant limestone town house, circa 1885, on 92nd Street between Fifth and Madison.

"Come back in an hour, Fergus," Jonathan said, as he emerged from the car.

"Very good, sir." The reply came in a lilting Galway Bay accent.

Jonathan walked up the five alabaster steps edged by an exquisite cast-iron railing with quatrefoil motif, and used the generous, well-shined brass door knocker. The maid answered. Roseanna was young and pretty and almost impossible to shock. On his account, Abigail had had to terminate Hazel, the censorious Scottish woman that had been with her for years. In this kind of situation, something had to give.

"The missus is waiting for you, sir," said Roseanna,

with a little smile. The overly genteel construction of her message sounded odd in her Central American tones.

"Thank you, Roseanna," Jonathan said.

He walked up the stairs. This was a beautiful house, a bit of old New York from the days of Edith Wharton and Henry James. Everything was tasteful and decorous; the furniture was all fine French and English antiques, passed down through the family for generations. The walls in the foyer and drawing room were hung with the most subtle mauve damask. Aubusson rugs covered the lustrous parquet floors.

At the top of the stairs, he headed left past the library toward Abigail's room. He knew the way. This relationship had been going on for two years. They first met at a meeting—a very heated meeting—of the Landmarks Commission. Abigail, the ex-wife of Hamish Forester, scion of an enormously wealthy New York family and currently ambassador to Peru, was a member of the commission. Jonathan was there to defend his plans to raze a rather moldy little brownstone on West 54th Street, a portion of which had once been home to the poet Edna St. Vincent Millay. Much emotional discussion was generated, with the immaculately cool Ms. Forester developing the most engaging flush along her pearly neck. To cool things off and repair bridges, Jonathan had invited Abigail to lunch the next day at The Quilted Giraffe. Over the chévre and maché salad, Jonathan felt her delicate hand touch his thigh. And the rest, as they say, was history.

He knocked on her door. There was no answer. She liked to hide and she liked him to find her. He had no complaints.

"Abigail?" he murmured. He looked in the dressing room and then, opening the bathroom door, he was struck by the haunting fragrance of jasmine with which she had perfumed her bath.

There she was, in the bath, her hair down, her beautiful breasts shining wetly. She looked at him, deliberately, silently, and then took a gold-plated razor and slowly, langorously, began to shave her pubic area. Immediately he felt an enormous swelling in his groin. As she watched him watching her, a teasing sort of smile grew on her sculpted lips.

"Jonathan," she said, in her flawlessly well-bred tones, the product of an education at The Madeira School and Vassar and the requisite year at the Sorbonne, "you look hot and tired. Would you care to join me?"

He stared at her and then he smiled. "Yes."

Slowly—for her benefit and, perhaps, for his—he disrobed. She watched him with the same sort of appraising eye she used at Sotheby's and David Webb. As he removed his pants, and his undershorts, exposing the full tale of his excitation, she revealed her own excitation in her eyes, the way they glittered, and her lips, they way they parted.

The temperature of the bath was perfect. It constantly amazed him how she managed to get everything so perfect. Her problem was that she was too perfect, but it wasn't a problem that concerned him right now.

"I've been waiting for you *all* morning," she said petulantly, as she nibbled on his lips.

"I couldn't have gotten here any sooner, Abigail," he said, touching the wet velvet of her breasts, putting his lips to her nipples, running a tongue around them.

She moaned as he played rough with her breasts. "No," she said. "I'm going to . . ."

"Don't you dare," he warned. "You'll come when I want you to come."

They went in and out of games of control—that's how they played. Their lips and tongues went everywhere, and she was lusting for him as she took him in her mouth, all of him, and the look of lust on that patrician face was incongruous and incredibly exciting. Taking her in his arms, he lifted her out of the bath. He laid her down on the fluffy yellow monogrammed Porthault bath sheet, and she took him in hand and put him inside of her, where the flow of her arousal had created a warmth that made him grit his teeth for fear of ending this all too soon.

"Do me rough, darling," she panted. "Do me rough." Yes, she liked it rough. He called her all the right names—names that, if she had heard them in the drawing room, would have caused her to cut the speaker dead—and she repaid him with a degree of attention and lubricity that he had seldom encountered before. He had her up on top of him, impaled on him, as he played with her breasts, and she was practically weeping with pleasure that was almost pain. Then he put her down again on the bath sheet and with slow, endless strokes, he brought her first to the pitch of utter ecstasy and then beyond, so that she was screaming her perfect head off, not caring what Roseanna would think, not even what people on the street would think.

When it was over, he fell into that sweet kind of stupor. Minutes—or was it hours?—later, she woke him, her face lit by a Cheshire cat grin.

"Lovely, darling," she said, running a faultlessly

groomed, coral-colored fingernail around his nipple. She was smoking a thin pink Nat Sherman cigarette, flavored with clove, and her hair hung around her face in tendrils, making her look like a pre-Raphaelite beauty.

Kissing her again on the breast, he rose, washed himself off, threw on some of the Hermes cologne that she kept on hand for him, and began to get dressed.

"Business as usual," she said with a smirk.

"All play and no work . . ."

"No, dearest. No one would ever have to worry about such a thing with you." She took another puff and threw her cigarette in the bathwater for Roseanna to dispose of. "When will I see you again?"

He reached into his coat pocket for his book. "Let's see. I'm in Atlantic City tomorrow and dinner with the Lieutenant Governor in the evening. Then the next day I'm off to Frankfurt for two days . . ."

"Frankfurt," she said, making a face. "Poor Jonathan."

"Thursday?" he said brightly.

"Same time? Same place?"

"Good enough," he said.

She gave him a deep, lingering kiss and then pulled back. "I'll keep it hot for you," she said lewdly, in those pearly tones, and he felt the hardening again.

"Got to go, luv," he said, giving her a peck on the cheek.

As he headed down the steps, Roseanna called out to him, her eyes sparkling. "Have a good day, Mister Broad."

The idea of a brief downstairs assignation occurred to him as he eyed the dark-complexioned young woman. No, he told himself. You cannot be all things to all people. "Thank you, Roseanna," he said, letting himself out.

There was the Bentley, with Fergus reading the *Wall Street Journal* behind the wheel. He, too, had become something of an investor in the year he had been working for the Broad Company. "Back to the office, sir?" asked Fergus.

"Yes," said Jonathan, as he sank down into the deep camel-colored leather upholstery.

As he sorted through his memos and interoffice correspondence, he thought of Stella, with whom he had not slept in two months, and Abigail, and Lolly Hunnicutt, and Roseanna, and all the women out there who could be his. *Make a life for yourself,* his father had warned. Ironic message, wasn't it, when he seemed to have everything in the world that every man wanted. The car sped down Fifth toward the sleek tower that was his.

3

SHE DIDN'T LIKE the water. Her ancestors were earth-bound, not sailors. But she was a good sport and she knew how to make the best of things.

Stella stretched out on the bed in the spacious but spare cabin of the *Pickle,* the 50-foot sailing vessel, moored at the 79th Street Boat Basin, of Wayne Mullins, whom she variously called Wayne, Waynie, Moon Mullins, and Big Boy. She had been seeing him on and off for six months now, ever since they'd met at a party for Bruce Springsteen in L.A. They'd seen each other across the room, and, wasting no time, met each other halfway. She liked the cut of his jib. He was very, very tall—6'6"—and he had a long face ending in a rakish pointed beard. His hands were huge, and you know what they say about men with big hands? Well, believe it. The only person in whom Stella could confide the intimate details of her affair was her hairdresser, a wild Southern queen named Billy Joe, and when she told him the dimensions of Wayne, she thought Billy Joe was going to expire from sheer envy.

"Stella, baby, you up?" groaned Wayne in his thick Oklahoma accent. He must have been something twenty years ago, Stella thought, when he was a boy wildcatting in the oil fields. She would sell her soul to have seen his twenty-year-old man-boy's chest, and the rest of him too.

"I'm up, Waynie," she said, as she sat in bed and brushed her hair. "But don't tell me you are again."

"You only live once," he cracked, making a grab for her.

She pretended to fight him off, raking his back with her nails. He loved her nails blood red and three inches long. One thing she could afford to buy herself were nails, so she took herself off to one of those nail clinics where they did a glue job that could fool your own natural mother.

"OK, cat," he hissed. "Stella the Cat. You like to play rough?"

He slapped her hard across the face. She gasped then, in earnest, and tried to rip and slash at his face with her talons. He grabbed her arms and pinned her down on the bed. She managed to sink her teeth into his bony shoulder. What tough meat he was, she thought—a tough old turkey, even if he was only 42.

He pulled her by the hair, forcing her to let go with her teeth. "Mmmmnh," he growled, deep in his throat, and then he quickly, stealthily invaded her with his very long forefinger, and she gasped again.

"You like that, baby?"

"Shut up and do it," she demanded.

He grinned and arranged her as he liked it, with her on all fours and him behind her. Then he started the savage thrusting that they both loved, and she felt him fill her to the breaking point, and then she was screaming, and then she was asleep once more. When she awoke, she saw that it was later than she thought. Why couldn't she be here forever? she wondered. Why couldn't she have him inside her forever?

She kissed him awake. He looked at her, first groggily and then with fondness. "Was good, Stellie," he said, with a shake of his head.

"I figured you liked it," she replied.

"I like everything about you, babe," he growled.

She smiled. In the last six months, they'd grown thick as thieves. It was good; it was right. Wayne was probably the best known corporate raider in the country; his name was in the business pages of the *Times* and the *Wall Street Journal* almost daily. In the last year, he had gained control of a handful—a fistful—of major corporations, and his personal wealth was staggering to contemplate. He probably made Jonathan look like a pauper, she thought, with that tingle of excitement that never left her, no matter how much money she had in the bank or in her pockets or around her neck. Some people on earth— some really stupid people—got all excited about hybrid tea roses or Maine sunsets or babies' bottoms. She got excited about money. She liked it in almost any form, but her favorites were negotiable bonds, stock certificates, and the real thing. Clean green money—she liked the look of it, the smell of it, the feel of it. She liked what it did for the complexion.

Now Wayne was a little different where money was concerned. He didn't dress like someone who had a lot of money; he didn't furnish his boat with gold-plated faucets. Money for him was a game, and he was the best high roller in the whole damn world. That's what she liked about him. She liked men with power. That's what had attracted her to Jonathan in the first place—that and the green stuff. But Jonathan was, at bottom, too nice a guy, and that bored her. He wanted her to be too decent and fine and respectable. She was a good actress, but there comes a time in the course of a day when you want to take off your make-up.

"We do make a good team, don't we?" Stella said. She was in no hurry to pull on her oversized black Kansai pullover with the tiger embossed on it. She had magnificent breasts, full, well formed, with lush dark nipples, and there was no rush to cover them.

"Come here," said Wayne.

"Now stop," Stella grinned. "We can't keep going on like this. I've got to get back to work."

"Screw work."

"Exactly—that's all you've got on your mind. Screw work."

He pulled back the sheets to expose himself. He was ready—and irresistible.

"Jesus," she said with a shudder. She moved over to him. Kneeling down, she took him in her hand and then her mouth. He groaned with great pleasure as she went about her business—a business she was very good at. She'd been very good at it for years. As a girl, she'd discovered a talent for it, and she made special friends—football heroes, teachers, neighbors—anyone who could help her. Too smart to accept large gifts, she accepted small ones. When she came to the city, it was more of the same. She told everyone she was an actress, but she didn't go to acting classes; she didn't have an agent. She did some modeling on Seventh Avenue and some print work. Some of the print work she shouldn't have done. It made her think now of Jerry Castriata, Fat Jerry. *Stella baby. Little Stella Nevins.* She wanted not to think of him. Instead

39

she thought of Wayne and the way he was groaning
and what he could do for her.

"Oh, babe. Oh, babe. You're the best, babe. You're
the best."

She *was* the best. That's what she needed to hear.
She concentrated and finished him off, and let the
sounds of his pleasure fill her ears like Mozart. "Oh,
babe," he said, pulling her into his arms and burying
his head between her breasts.

"We make a good team, sweetie," she whispered.
"We've got places to go."

"Blow in my ear," he grinned, "and I'll follow you
to the ends of the earth."

"Not that far, Waynie, but thanks anyway." She
pulled out one of her Ultrathins and lit up, puffing
away as he grinned at her.

"I never met a woman like you before, Stella," he
said. "You're in a class by yourself."

"I know," she said, and they laughed. She liked
him—everything about him. They could do great
things together.

"I really ought to be going," she said, stretching
langorously. "Back to the shop."

"They won't miss you," he said, reaching out for
her.

"Oh, yes. They're down a hand," she said cannily.

"How so?"

"David Broad. The old gray stallion ain't what he
used to be," she said, getting up and pulling on her
very fine lingerie.

"What do you mean?" he asked, with a note of
tension in his voice. She knew that nothing excited
him more than the inside track, and she liked the idea
of playing with him. It gave her a thrill of her own.

"David's looking like he's been passed the Black Spot, and Jonathan knows it. Poor Jonathan—he's shaking in his boots. What will life be like without Daddy?"

"Come on," said Wayne, reaching for his Marlboros. "It's not like Papa David's sitting around calling the shots."

"That's true," she allowed. "He's not the tactician. But—and it's a big but—he holds Jonathan up. Wait and see—if David kicks the bucket, Jonathan's going to go into a tailspin. And others in his organization, who shall be nameless, will be looking to make their move."

"Like you?" Wayne smirked.

"Up yours, Charlie," she smirked back. "I'm talking about Jonathan's allegedly loyal aides-de-camp. Hang around and see how loyal they'll be."

"So then the picture you're painting makes the Broad Company seem like it's ripe for takeover," Wayne said thoughtfully.

She saw the wheels turning and she felt her own flush of excitement again, as if she were on her way to an inside straight.

"This is interesting," he said, livening up. "You really think that Jonathan is going to fall apart?"

She pulled the sweater over her tousled mane of black hair. "Got to run, sweetie," she said, giving him a deep kiss. "I'll call you."

"Stella!" he shouted, but she was out the door, with a great big smile on her face.

She had just enough time to shower, change into something a little more appropriate, and high-tail it to the restaurant.

"Good afternoon, Madame Broad," said Jean-Paul, the maitre'd.

"Good afternoon, J.P.," she replied, and headed for her usual table.

They loved her at Le Cirque; she out-Biancaed Bianca, and she brought a real sense of drama and glamor with her. She strode through the glittering room and nodded to her acquaintances, moving so that people would watch her. She moved like a panther—a panther who'd just made a kill but was hungry nonetheless.

"Oogie," she said, extending her hand to her luncheon date, Oogie—né Oliver—Banks.

Oogie rose—he came up to Stella's sternum—and she bent down to offer her cheek, which he air-kissed. "Stella, you look ravishing," he said in his little hoarse-breathy voice with the words ending in a sort of metallic whine. "You should be starring in a Joe Papp production of *Carmen*."

She didn't quite know how to take that, so she smiled absently and sat down in the plush seat. As she took off her turquoise kid gloves, she ordered a Stolichnaya with a chaser of Ramosa water. "I hope I haven't kept you long, Oogie."

"Only as long as you should have, pet," he twinkled.

She patted his cheek and he lit up like a lightbulb. He was somewhere in the vicinity of sixty, and had one leg shorter than the other, a bald pate as shiny as melamac, and about as much virility as a Mexican hairless. Nobody quite knew what he did, except that he had a lot of money left to him by his father, who'd been a lifetime with Lazard Frères, and that he dabbled in interior design and acted as a consultant to

Vogue. His other claim to fame was that he was very good chums with Nancy Reagan. Indeed, whenever Nancy came to New York, she lunched at Le Cirque with Oogie. Consequently, to be seen at lunch at Le Cirque with Oogie was a feather in one's cap—and an egret feather, not one of your turkey numbers.

"The clams smell vile today," Oogie cackled, rolling his eyes.

"Never touch the things myself," Stella confessed.

"No. Why would you? A girl from the Midwest—America's heartland—what would you know about shellfish?" he said.

She glanced at him. It was going to be one of those sorts of lunches, she thought, all bitchery and sarcasm. Cool out, Stella, she warned herself. "We always had the catch of the sea flown out to us," Stella said, as she reached in her bag for her cigarettes.

"Oh, did you?" he said archly.

She didn't like his tone. It sounded like he'd done some research on her. Dot Nevins and her duty shoes and her common-law husband Adolph *schtupping* the kid were not meant to be the talk of the town. "You look marvelous, Oogie," she said, changing the subject. "Where have you been?"

"Oh, my," he said, biting his lip delicately, "let me see. All over. Acapulco—at Gloria's (that was doyenne Gloria Guinness), then I looked at some ruins in the interior—"

"How was that?" she said, between puffs.

He rolled his eyes. *"Hated* the ruins, *loved* the Indians," he leered. "Then to L.A. At L'Hermitage . . ."

"Lovely, isn't it?"

"Oh, yes. Everyone wanted me to stay with them,

but I said no, no, no, no! In L.A. I need my rest and I need my privacy."

And you need your boys, she thought, smiling through the smoke.

"And you, my dearest? I want you to know I cried bitter tears missing your opening the other day. Everyone said it was *absolutely* breathtaking."

"Sweet of them," she murmured. "Why don't I take you through it after lunch?"

"Oh, that would be lovely," he said, "but I'm running down to the capital at three."

"Another time," she said sweetly.

They both ordered the fish and the arugula salad.

"Now tell me," he said, leaning forward conspiratorially, "what's put the bloom in *your* cheeks, my girl?"

She smiled noncommittally. "It must be the excitement of the Palace opening," she said.

"And I'm Dolores Del Rio," he snapped. "Come, pet. You have the look of a woman getting a little something on the side. And why you would, when you have that delicious hunk of Jonathan, is the great mystery. Elucidate, sweetie, right now."

She felt something twist inside her—the enormous, palpable serpent of her anger. She wanted to take the cutlery and drive it into his toad face. But she kept on smiling, even though she knew it wasn't good for her health. "You do have a vivid imagination, Oogie. You should write one of those great big best-sellers."

"Oh, but I intend to, pet," he said, his mouth full of fish, "and you're going to star in it. Now hear me out. Rumor has it that you and a certain raider—and I don't mean Harrison Ford, lovely as that would be—are having it on. Response?"

"I don't know what you're talking about," she said

determinedly. "And I don't think I want to hear any more of this."

He snorted. "Stelllla," he said, drawing out her name patronizingly, as if addressing a naughty child. "Don't go all virginal on me, darling. That would be a supreme act of miscasting, like the late great Barbara Payton going for a Joan Fontaine role."

There was a silence, which he filled with his chewing. "I don't think I know who Barbara Payton was," she said icily.

"Oh, no? A serious lapse, pet. She was this terrific 1940s blonde. Played with Jimmy Cagney in *Kiss Tomorrow Goodbye*. The one Franchot Tone and Tom Neal almost killed each other over? Before your time but oh, she was something. Like many a Forties bombshell, however, she fizzled out, and I think when she died she was working as a . . . pardon the expression . . . hooker."

She would have liked to slap him across the face. Or throw a martini all over him. She would have liked to discipline him, as if he were a messy little pug who had pooped on the white carpeting. But she couldn't. He had the disposition and reputation of a puff adder and he could destroy her standing, and she had worked too hard for it.

"You're very inquisitive, Oogie," she said coyly, "and I hate to disappoint you . . ."

"Cut the cutes," he said viciously. "Are you fucking Wayne Mullins or not?"

If she lied to him, she would be finished. He wanted her in the palm of his hand and he was good at that sort of thing and he didn't like to be betrayed. On the other hand, if she told him the truth—or, at least, if she didn't deny it—he would feel that he was her confidante, that she was one of "his girls," and maybe, just maybe, he wouldn't betray her.

"Is there anything going on in New York that you don't know about?" she said, putting her hand on his.

He stared at her. If he were capable of getting an erection, she had the feeling that this was the time. "Good girl," he said with his little metallic whine. "Now, for the details. What is the great Wayne Mullins like in the sack?"

She took a long draught of her Stolichnaya. As she did so, she looked around. All the rich and famous— were they all looking at her? Little Stella Nevins, what are you doing here in the middle of us? Is that what they were thinking? Well, screw them and their mothers.

"Oogie," she said, flushed from the vodka and the admission, watching his beady little eyes glimmer with anticipation, "he's one of your last *real* men . . ."

She and Oogie kissed goodbye in front of the restaurant and she walked back the few blocks to her office. It was a crisp fall day and everything was perfect, except that she had had too much to drink and she was in a real bitch, a witch's brew, of a mood. Her boots were thunderclaps on the sidewalk and she pushed against people as she made her way.

When she got up to the 27th floor, she brushed past her secretary, Diane, and slammed the door of her office. Furiously, she took a tiny Steuben pigeon and smashed it against the wall. After a few moments, she calmed down. There was work to do, and she was glad of it. She buzzed Diane to come in.

With some timidity, Diane entered. She was a

mousy young woman, a graduate of Bryn Mawr and a dropout from the Yale School of Architecture, Stella's third—and definitely not last—secretary of the year.

"Messages," said Stella, putting out her hand, snapping her long, blood red nails.

Diane handed her the sheaf of pink message slips. Stella leafed through them—half social, half business —and then stopped, with her heart stopping too, as she read one of them. Jerry Castriata. She looked up at Diane. "This is marked urgent," she said sternly. "Why?"

Diane peered through her horn-rimmed glasses. "Oh, yes. Mr. Castriata. He was most insistent that you call him by five. Shall I get him for you?"

"You'll get him for me when I ask you to get him for me," she said, and watched the moon-pale girl turn pink. "Did he say . . . what he wished to speak with me about?" she probed.

"No, I'm sorry, Mrs. Broad. I tried to get that information from him but . . ."

"You tried, you tried, but. *But.* Now there's the word that defines you, Diane. Thank you. I'll place this call myself."

Diane nodded submissively and withdrew from the office. Twerp, Stella thought furiously. She looked at the name on the message slip. Jerry Castriata. What a name. What a fat, greasy, disgusting name. 713-8883. Even his phone number was disgusting.

She ran a hand through her hair. What did he want? No—what a stupid question. She knew what he wanted. Eight years ago, when she was broke, she modeled for him. He had run an ad in the *Voice*: '*Artistic models wanted for exciting photographic venture.*' A loft in the flower district. A space heater.

Another woman, Filipina, with breasts shaped like Bartlett pears. A lot of coke. A *lot* of coke. Dunkin Donuts and coffee and Gallo burgundy. She got smashed and did everything they wanted. She did to the Filipina woman and she let the Filipina woman do to her. There were costumes too—leather ones, with martial-looking hats. She felt herself break into a cold sweat. He had come back to haunt her, to ruin her life, all for the $200 she'd earned that night.

What should she do? She had this funny impulse to ask Jonathan. She didn't love Jonathan—she never really had—but she had always felt, somehow, that she could rely on him. When they first got together, she'd loved playing the role of the one who needed to be taken care of. Jonathan was so comfortable being the taker-carer, the strong one, the solver. In some ways, it was really a damned shame that she didn't love him.

She picked up the phone—something she rarely did herself—and dialed the number. Her heart was pounding hard as she waited for him to answer, and then he did.

"Stella, baby?" came the voice.

She felt something sink inside of her. Did he have no one else who called him? Did he have such big plans for little Stella Nevins?

"What do you want, Jerry?" she said, forcing herself to control her voice.

"Just wanted to reconnect, Stella baby . . ."

"Stop calling me that!" she said shrilly, and then knew she'd made a mistake.

"OK, Mrs. Broad. I'll stop calling you that."

Money. Of course. But the question was how much?

And what would she be getting for it and where would it end?

"OK, Jerry. Let's get this over with. State your business."

He laughed, very loud and much too long, maddeningly long. "You're a pip, Stella. Always were. Now listen," he said seriously. "I like primates, understand?"

She didn't understand. She didn't know what the hell he was talking about. "Primates?" she said.

"Love to watch 'em. Monkeys, chimps, gibbons, baboons. My favorites. I want you to meet me tomorrow at ten A.M. in the Ape House at the Bronx Zoo. You can't miss it. It's right across from the reptile house, a stone's throw from the World of Darkness."

"The Bronx Zoo?" she said. "Are you crazy? I'm not going to the goddamn Bronx Zoo . . ."

"What's the matter with the Bronx Zoo, Stell? All your high society ladies give money there. Enid Haupt and Mrs. Astor and all them. Don't you want to be like them?" he chortled.

"You son of a bitch . . ."

"Ten o'clock tomorrow morning, Mrs. Broad," he said soberly. "In front of the mountain gorillas. I'll have a Nikon around my neck in case you forgot what I look like."

"Listen, you . . ." she began, but then he hung up and she was left with the dial tone. She hung up the phone and went into the bathroom to wash off her face with cool water.

4

NOBODY MADE EGGS like Lucy, thought Roxy Monahan as she sat in Sal & Lucy's Waterside Vista Cafe, about to pierce the most perfect poached egg in existence. Damn Craig Claiborne. Damn Gael Greene. Damn all those yuppies who went in search of eggs benedict or eggs sardou or eggs florentine. They wouldn't know a good egg if they had a chicken for an uncle. But Lucy—ah, Lucy knew eggs. She had her own distributor come in mornings from a Jersey poultry farm and then she lovingly took the eggs in her big capable hands and then she worked her Lucy magic on them. Bless Lucy and bless the Waterside Vista Cafe and bless the chickens and the eggs, Roxy thought as she cut into the yolk and watched it drip and wiped it up with the piece of rye toast that was about as "complex" a food as she wanted at six-thirty in the morning.

"Pass the salt," Ryan said, his mouth full of bacon.

"Don't talk with your mouth full," said Roxy, her own mouth full, as she passed the salt to her brother. She watched Ryan—the youngest of her four brothers —salt his bacon. "Look at him, Pop," she said to her father, "your son is salting bacon. Did you ever see such a lunatic, as if there wasn't any heart disease running through the family like a brushfire, as if you yourself didn't have angina and weren't on a low-salt diet and weren't sitting there eating oatmeal?"

"Our sister the lawyer," muttered Brendan, her oldest brother, two years her senior. "The gift of gab incarnate."

She hit him on the head with her rolled-up *Times.* "You're not so bad in the gab department yourself, Monahan," she snarled at her brother.

"Don't let her rag you, Brendan," piped in Dennis, a middle brother. He was the one she particularly loved, maybe because his clubfoot made him more vulnerable than the others. Her fourth brother, Joseph, was a priest right here in Red Hook and had found his own kind of love. She reached across the table and landed a blow with the rolled-up newspaper on Dennis's head.

"Well, now, ain't this a lovely sight?" said her father, in a brogue that hadn't diminished one whit since Edmund Francis Patrick Monahan's departure from Galway forty years earlier. "The deputy commissioner of the waterfront assaulting innocent men with an unregistered weapon."

Roxy held the paper aloft and made as if to go at her father, but he grabbed her hand and held it with a comic fierceness. "Always was a little hellion, always will be. Well, you're not too old nor too big in your boots to be over my knee, Roxy Monahan."

"You let that girl alone now, Edmund Monahan," said Lucy, coming over with some rich, piping hot coffee. She was Italian, but a natural mimic, and took

51

on a language of straight Galwayese when waiting on the Monahans, as she had done every morning for the last quarter-decade.

"Don't involve yourself in family affairs, me girl, and you won't get yourself into trouble," he cautioned Lucy.

"And this one ain't like me own?" Lucy said, hands on hips, glaring at Edmund.

It was true. Ever since her mother died, when Roxy was nine, Lucy had been like a second mother to her. Roxy had grown up in a fourth-floor railroad flat two doors down from the Waterside Vista where the Monahan men still lived, and it was Lucy who'd cut Roxy's flame red bangs, it was Lucy who'd sewed Roxy's prom dress, it was Lucy to whom she turned when the mysteries of womanhood descended on her tomboyish person. "Yeah, Pop," said Roxy, putting an arm around Lucy's ample waist. "And don't ever forget it."

This was home for Roxy. The second booth on the right. Lucy's. Red Hook. Every morning she left her apartment, a big converted loft on Pearl Street in an old tool and die factory, and went down for breakfast at Lucy's with Pop and the boys before they went out on the *Galway Bay*. It was a randy old tug, short and squat, built just like Pop in fact. Roxy's tall, willowy frame came from her mother, as did her red hair and green eyes. The height differential as well as her mother's frequent, if benign, needling of her husband, caused the two of them to be known in the neighborhood as Maggie and Jiggs. Edmund Monahan had never gotten over his wife's death. The tug became his constant companion, and the three boys were as hooked into it as he was. None of them had married yet, and maybe they never would. They were a fierce sort of brood, the Monahans were, thought Roxy, and it would be hard for another woman to enter the clan.

"So what have you got on your agenda today, Roxy?" her father asked, scowling at his unsalted oatmeal.

"I'm meeting with Jonathan Broad," she said between sips of the reviving coffee.

"Jonathan Broad?" said Ryan. "Never heard of him."

"You never heard of anyone who didn't play ball," said Brendan, shaking his head contemptuously.

It was true, Roxy thought. Ryan was not exactly a whiz kid. He had wanted to be a major league ballplayer, but had only made it to the minors, and there his career was cut down by a series of injuries and physical ailments—bone spurs, torn ligaments, and the like. Roxy worried about his spirit, but he was such a guileless person that he would probably make out okay.

"Jonathan Broad is today's robber baron," Brendan explained. Brendan was the intellectual among the brothers—except, of course, for Joseph, who was Jesuit trained. Brendan would have made a fine lawyer himself, or a journalist, but Pop had wanted him on the boat, and there he was. Because she was a woman, it had been easier for Roxy to escape.

"Now, Brendan," said Pop, "don't go calling names in your rabble-rousing way, if you please."

"I call a spade a spade," said Brendan. "The man is a robber baron. He takes from the poor and gives to the rich. What's your business with him, Roxy?"

"He's got something on the drawing boards he calls River Park," she said, making desultory circles in the egg yolk with her toast.

"River Park?" said Ryan ingenuously. "Sounds nice."

"The lad doesn't mind talking, does he?" cracked Dennis, who was looking over the racing form. He was the rascal among the brothers, going in for horses and prostitutes and the occasional big splurge in Atlantic City. He needed a lot of bravado, Roxy realized, to make up for the clubfoot that had kept him from being a big-shot at high school like his brothers.

"Well, what's wrong with a park?" asked Ryan, defensive and turning red.

"It's not a park in the sense that we know the term, Ryan," Roxy said patiently. "It's a huge development that will stretch from Hell's Kitchen up to the 79th Street Boat Basin. There'll be malls, park space, condominiums, office space . . ."

"Condominiums," growled Brendan, who drank his coffee pitch black and smoked eight Chesterfield cigarettes during each breakfast. "The vilest word to enter into the English language in the last half-century."

"That's a little rough, Brendan," Roxy said.

"Maybe to you," he challenged. "With your fancy 'loftspace' and all that bunk."

That stung. She was a little self-conscious about the loft even though she loved its light and its space and its comfort. Brendan had always been competitive— as a lawyer, she was doing what he wanted to do in the best of all possible worlds—and he knew how to zing her. If she didn't love him, and love the way his mind

54

worked, it would be bad between them. But of all her brothers, he was the one to whom she turned for advice about her work, for he was as well informed as anyone she knew and had a razor-sharp mind and a built-in bullshit detector that never faltered.

"Well, what's this Broad fellow want to do?" Pop asked.

"What do you think, Pop?" Brendan said. "He wants to take the waterfront and he wants to turn it into one great big . . . boutique! Take your boat and turn it into a nice little floating Haagen-Dazs shop."

Pop's eyes narrowed. "What's this Hag and Dots?" he said suspiciously. "Sounds foreign."

Roxy couldn't help laughing. Dear old Pop. The only ice cream he ever put between his lips was Breyer's vanilla.

"And you, Lucy," said Brendan to Lucy, who looked even more confused than Ryan, "you could do the whole place over. Lots of ferns and hanging plants, dearie, and gotta change the menu. Quiche. Lots of quiche. Dinty Moore's quiche."

Roxy giggled. Brendan, like many an Irishman, had a wonderful satiric bent. It was all lost on Lucy, but Roxy could appreciate the way her brother zeroed in on the menace of gentrification.

"Well, you listen to me, sister," said Brendan, suddenly serious. "You better get on the tail of that fat cat, understand? It's your duty to this family and this neighborhood to shoot down River Park." He grimaced. "The name itself fairly gives me the shudders. River Park," he spat out. "This harbor's not a park! It's the blood of this city! There are things on the bottom of this harbor that would take your breath away. Dinosaur bones, treasure, booty, corpses. You tell your Mr. Jonathan Broad that this ain't no place for fancy folk to try on pretty frocks and fancy cowboy boots. Now will you do that, girl?"

She stared at all the people she loved—her father, her brothers, Lucy. She looked around the Waterside Vista Cafe, with its wonderful ambiance that hadn't changed in three decades, its rotting old decorative fishing nets, the mermaid figurehead on the wall taken off an old Greek sailing vessel, the blackboard with today's specials representative of the great polyglot cuisine that showed the ethnic influences of the Irish, the Italians, the Poles, the Scandinavians, the Greeks, all part of this rich, raffish, fantastic neighborhood. Damn Jonathan Broad, she thought. "Don't worry," she assured them, sipping the dregs of her coffee, "I'm on the job."

It was cold on the water. It was late September but you could feel the autumn in the air; the city, waking up, had a steelier look and there were puffy charcoal clouds in the sky. The gulls, feeling the cold in their pinfeathers, in their bones, cawed with a sense of urgency that got under your skin and made you pull your coat closer around you.

She sat in the rear, watching the wake of the *Galway Bay*, sipping from the cup of coffee that Lucy always sent her away with. She watched her three brothers go about their work, appreciating the beauty of strong, healthy young men engaged in honest labor. She had a problem, she knew, with the men she worked with, the "right" men. Because she wasn't bad to look at—all right, under pressure she'd confess that most men found her damned good to look at—she got more than her share of attention in the office. She was

surrounded by WASPy boys, Harvard graduates like
her, with family money behind them and the full
intention of starting out in the public sector and
working their way up in politics. All of these boys—
and she thought of them as boys, even though they
were in the vicinity of 30, as she was—carried tennis
or squash racquets with them to work and had perfect
blond locks and chiseled features and horn-rimmed
glasses and great bodies underneath their Brooks
Brothers suits. She supposed there were few women in
this city of unavailable men who would not jump at
the chance to bed down with this bunch. But she
wasn't one of them. She liked a man who could work
with his hands, who didn't chatter, who had a bit of
roughness to his beard and maybe some dirt under his
nails. But those men were scared off by her. She was,
after all, the deputy commissioner of the waterfront.

She had always scared off men. As a girl, she'd been
consistently the best student in her class. It just came
easy to her, that was all. Math, science, English,
history, debating—it was all gravy to her. When she
graduated high school, valedictorian and president of
her class, she was offered a full scholarship to Harvard. Now that was an experience, going up to Boston, knowing more than ever what it was to be potato
famine Irish among the Brahmin. And there, not only
was she Irish, but she had a New Yawk accent that
made Geraldine Ferraro sound like Vanessa Red-
grave. She still had it and, she thought as she gazed
out at the New York City skyline that thrilled her no
matter how many times she saw it, she wouldn't get
rid of it for anything. After Harvard, Phi Beta Kappa,
magna cum laude, she went to Harvard Law School.
She discovered that she loved the law, the sense of it,

the power, the rightness of it. She loved having an appropriate place to put her assertiveness. When she graduated, editor of the *Law Review,* she'd been courted by every law firm in New York: Mudge, Rose; Rogers & Wells; Cleary, Gottlieb; even the super-WASP bastion of Sullivan & Cromwell. Even though she was a woman, even though she was Irish, even though she talked like someone from Red Hook, everyone wanted her. The salaries they offered were startling, the promises compelling; the lunches they plied her with were flattering and filling; and in the end she said no. No, no, no. She didn't want to work for corporate clients, searching for ways to make the rich richer.

She decided instead to accept a decidedly modest offer from the small maritime law firm of O'Brian, Hutchins & Swenson. From there, it hadn't been a far jump to her present position. The mayor, noting her incipient value as a media figure, decided that a tall, good-looking, redheaded woman maritime lawyer with a New Yawk accent was just the thing for the post of deputy commissioner of the waterfront. She had held it down for two years now, with bigger and better things in sight.

"A touch of chill in the air today, eh, Roxy?" Pop said, as he sat down beside her.

"Just a touch, Pop, but you can feel it right into your bones, can't you?"

He took her hand. "Cold hand," he said.

"Warm heart," she complied.

"Lovely heart," he said, bringing her hand to his lips. "You're a lovely woman, Roxy . . ."

In need of a fine man. Here it came, the get married-and-have-children spiel. She was going to have to start taking the subway to work if he kept this up.

"You'd make some man very . . ."

"Come on, Pop. You've got three sons who could also give you grandchildren. Don't get on my back alone, will you?"

"Now don't get your dander up, girl. I'm just making a simple point . . ."

"Yeah. Very simple. Barefoot and pregnant."

"Now," he blustered, "you never let a person finish a sentence. Just like your mother."

She was about to open her mouth again, but instead, she sipped at the coffee.

"I'm just suggesting that you're thirty years old now. A woman who wants to have a family's got to start thinking about such things at that age. Now I know there's plenty of young men has got to be interested in a beautiful young woman such as yourself, but I don't see nor hear signs of it, so all I'm doing is . . ."

". . . is asking what gives," she interrupted, unable to resist. "Well, Pop, the answer is nothing gives. I haven't met any man that I want to make a life with, let alone spend more than a few evenings with. Most of them are childish or gay or looking for some kind of action I can't give them. So you'll just have to sit tight, OK? And try someone else for a change. How about Ryan? He seems like the marrying kind, given half a chance."

Edmund turned his searching gaze on his daughter —his bright blue eyes reminded her sometimes of lighthouse beacons—and then impulsively reached out to hug her. "Don't think I'm criticizing you, Roxy," he said, patting her red hair. "You're the best

59

daughter I could ever imagine. I couldn't be more proud of a child than I am of you. It's just that life is a long and lonely haul, me girl, and I want you to be happy in it."

"I am, Pop," she said, squeezing back some tears. "Believe me, I am."

As Edmund walked back to the bridge, Roxy stared out at the harbor, thinking of all the place names that were foreign to 99 per cent of the city's population but as familiar to her as the back of her hand. Wallabout Bay. Buttermilk Channel. These were the avenues she knew best in the city, these and the streets of Red Hook. Maybe I'm out of step, she thought, as they neared Peck Slip where they would drop her off. Maybe I *should* give a damn about quiche and cowboy boots and condos.

No, she told herself, looking out at the incredible harbor that the Dutch had discovered hundreds of years ago, the hub and the reason for this city being what it was. This would not become a rich man's playground, diminished and ruined. Let Pop worry about a man for me, she thought as she pulled her coat closer against the chill autumn air. I'll worry about the future of the city I love.

She looked out the window of the office she hated on the 58th floor of the World Trade Center. She was sure she felt the tower sway in the wind, and the whole idea of being the deputy waterfront commissioner from way up here rather than from some little tin shack on the waterfront itself seemed absurd .

She took a sip of coffee—too much coffee; she really should get into drinking herbal tea, but rose hips didn't get her motor going—and began speaking into the dictaphone.

"Captain Stavros Theodorokis, Olympia Shipping Lines, address, etc. Dear Captain Theodorokis, in response to your question regarding . . ."

"Roxy," rang in Dolores, her secretary, "it's Peter Emmeroth from the *Times* on 21."

She picked up. "Peter," she said. "How are you?"

"Not bad, Roxy," he said. They were friends—regular dinner companions who enjoyed each other's company, except that Peter had a really serious drinking problem. That was the way with all the men she might have been interested in—they were all trouble in one way or the other. Or else they were married. Or else they were gay. It wasn't her fault! she wanted to scream when her father or Lucy or one of her brothers got on her.

"So?" she said. "Is this personal or professional?"

"Professional, luv," he laughed. "I need a statement from you about the new guidelines the EPA has set down regarding maritime transport of toxic materials."

"Give me an hour," she shot back.

"Long enough for you to formulate something appropriately bureaucratic?" he cracked.

The EPA guidelines were beyond the pale. The transport of toxic materials through the New York City harbor was the stuff of her nightmares, but she wasn't ready to see those words on page one of the *Times*. "An hour, Peter," she said, signing off.

She felt the beginnings of a headache. Allergies, she told herself, even though, on some level, she knew that it had to do with the pressures of her job. She walked over to the water cooler, popped a couple of Extra Strength Tylenols, and tried to will it away.

"You don't play squash, do you, Roxy?" asked Talbot Morrison, coming up behind her. A lawyer in charge of foreign shipping concerns, he was 6'2", built like a Calvin Klein model, had a face that would make Robert Redford nervous about the competition, and an educational and social pedigree that would wow them back in Red Hook. She covered her mouth with her hand, yawned a little, and shook her head. "No, Talbot. I don't play squash."

"Corking good game," he said with a boyish smile.

"I'm sure it is." Hadn't they had this conversation before? And why wouldn't he leave her alone?

"I'd love to introduce you to it . . ."

"Talbot, that's very nice of you, but, believe it or not, I have no time for games. I have no time for squash, for jogging, for working out on a Nautilus, for exercise of any sort."

He smiled at her, the kind of smile that announced that no matter what she said to him, he still found her irresistibly fascinating. "You really shouldn't neglect your bodily needs."

"Thanks anyway, Talbot," she said, brushing past him.

At one, she ate a quickie roast beef sandwich while Dolores, twenty pounds overweight, ate a Le Chocolat yogurt and complained about her boyfriend Dominic's mother. Then she had to gear up for the main event of the day: her meeting with Jonathan Broad and his associate, Sidney Farrell. The River Park project plans had wound up on her desk a few weeks ago, and last week she had gotten off a memo to Sidney Farrell pointing out a major problem with the project's conception: what it would do to the 68th Street harbor facility. This was a tug slip that the Broad Company had evidently overlooked in their planning, or had perhaps regarded as far more expendable than a David's Cookies outlet on the waterfront. Roxy had done her best to control her anger over the Broad Company's presumption, but evidently her anger had spilled out in her stinging letter. In any event, it was sufficient to get Mr. Jonathan Broad, the mighty *Wunderkind* himself, in to see her.

She gathered her papers and headed toward the conference room. As she passed the glassed-in office of her boss, she glanced at her reflection in the glass. Nice dress, bought at Sym's last fall. A little short? So what—she couldn't worry about hem lengths.

She entered the conference room and found the two men already seated. She couldn't ignore the injection of adrenalin that shot through her, coming face to face with Jonathan Broad, whose power and sheer *chutzpah* was already legendary. "Gentlemen, Roxanne Monahan," she announced, extending a firm hand. She felt the two men appraise her, particularly Broad, whose eyes seemed to convey a veiled amusement, making her feel like a little girl dressed up in her mother's clothes.

They got down to business right away. "You've had time to digest my memo, gentlemen?" she asked.

"Yes, Ms. Monahan, we have," said Jonathan coolly.

"And?" said Roxy, after a pause.

"Frankly, I found it rather combative," said Jonathan with a smile.

He was condescending to her. She dug in, trying her best not to break down in anger.

"I think what Jonathan means, Ms. Monahan, is that we should all try to feel like we're on the same side here."

"Oh, is that what you mean, Mr. Broad?" she said.

"Yes, that's what I mean," he said, with a coolly ironic smile. "And please—call me Jonathan."

He was smooth, she thought. And very good looking, better in person than in photographs. In the flesh, he had a youthful, vigorous quality, and his graceful frame and commanding manner were certainly not qualities she was immune to. Sidney Farrell, on the other hand, was getting on her nerves from the start. His thighs were going up and down nervously in the manner of an overanxious adolescent boy and his thick spectacles kept slipping down his nose.

"The River Park concept is fantastic," Sidney Farrell said. "Jonathan's got amazing vision. It's a gift to the city."

She loathed the fawning tone. What sort of man would surround himself with this kind of yes-man? "That could be debated, Mr. Farrell," she said in measured tones. "The park space allotted in the plan seems to be a rather small part of the parcel."

"Do you think so?" Jonathan said. "Actually, River Park will increase the total New York City park area by three per cent."

"You don't say," she replied indifferently, resenting his silly statistics. "But, in any case, that's not what we're here to discuss. We're here to discuss Slip #27. Which the Broad Company, as manifested in the River Park plan, seems to regard as utterly unnecessary to our waterfront."

"Ms. Monahan," said Sidney sweatily, "we're still at the stage where things can be adjusted . . ."

The message being *Don't be a hard-nose. Be a game-player, baby. Don't take it all so seriously.* Because she worked in waterfront, people automatically assumed she had a permanently greased palm. But it wasn't the case, and maybe she worked too hard, too severely, to convey the impression that it wasn't the case. And maybe—because she was a woman—she worked too hard to convey the impression that she was playing by her own set of rules, that she wasn't part of the clubhouse. The result was that she found herself in a bind with little room to breathe and headaches creeping up behind her eyes. "It's my job, Mr. Farrell, not to make any adjustments that will affect the life of the harbor . . ."

"The life of the harbor is what River Park is all about," Jonathan interjected quietly.

"Is it indeed, Mr. Broad?" she said, pointedly using his surname. She was feeling angry and she wasn't entirely sure why. He was polite and smooth and unruffled and everything she wasn't. She felt like the last in a long line of chronic Irish donnybrookers and suddenly she wanted to show Jonathan Broad just how good a scrapper she was. Maybe this wasn't the most professional behavior in the world—but she couldn't do a damned thing about it.

"River Park is just what this city needs, Ms. Monahan," said Sidney Farrell. "It's to no one's advantage to stall it with boondoggling. This is the most important civic project since . . . since . . ."

Since what? she thought. The Roman Forum? She didn't like these people. She didn't like their expensive suits and their expensive colognes and their whole mind-sets. "The most important civic project since Westway?" she said pointedly.

65

"Roxanne," Jonathan said, with great patience, "I hope you're not condemning this project without due trial . . ."

"I'm condemning nothing. I'm simply reviewing the situation, as my job demands."

"Of course. But I wouldn't want you to lose sight of the fact that River Park could be a great thing for our city . . ."

"What exactly is your understanding of *our* city, Mr. Broad?" Roxy asked, unable to keep the edge out of her voice. "The young professionals who are moving into luxury housing down on Battery Park? Or the young professionals who are taking over Clinton?" She didn't want to use the word 'yuppie' but it was clear whom she meant. "Or is it the indigenous neighborhood people of Red Hook and Lower Manhattan and the West Side who have been dying to have a Laura Ashley and a Ferragamo on their block?"

Jonathan's face tightened. "The city is changing. And change can be a positive thing . . ."

"It can be a very positive thing for a lucky few who think they have the alchemist's trick of turning dross into gold."

Jonathan considered the remark and then grinned. "Alchemists have never really had a very easy time of it with the petty bureaucrats, have they?" He rose to his full imposing height. "I trust we've taken up enough of your valuable time today. Come, Sidney. Let's go."

Sidney shuffled his papers into his briefcase and followed Jonathan. He turned to Roxy in a conciliatory fashion. "I'm sure we're all going to be able to work this out."

Silently she watched them go. This would no doubt

get back to the commissioner, who would be less than thrilled about putting the great Jonathan Broad's nose out of joint. "He's done a lot for the city," she could just hear him saying. And the city's done a lot for his bank account, she fumed.

Heading back to her office, lost in thought, she didn't even notice Talbot Marriner. He stationed himself in front of her and she bumped into him, rudely thrust from her reverie.

"Penny for your thoughts," he grinned.

"Buzz off," she snapped and walked on, leaving him astonished in her wake. She was in a mood to slay dragons and, what was worse, she had the awful feeling that she wouldn't be able to get Jonathan Broad out from under her skin.

5

THE MORNING SUN hung outside the eastern bank of windows as if it were a private bauble. In the breakfast room, which was all glass on three sides, suspended beyond the frame of the tower, Jonathan momentarily put down the *Wall Street Journal* and looked at the beds of hibiscus plants that flowered profusely in shades of red and pink, the mini-grove of dwarf citrus plants, many in blossom and in fruit, and the exquisite assortment of flowering cacti. He couldn't have had a more beautiful planting of flowers in Palm Beach, he realized, thanks to Mizoguchi, his wizardly interior landscaper. So what was the problem? What more could he want?

Stella sat at the other end of the table, reading WWD and *Interview,* wearing a silk robe in the lustrous pinkish white color of a freshwater pearl. Her long sleek legs and glimpses of her beautiful breasts showed beneath the shimmering fabric. "Ha!" she snorted. "Look at that fat bitch Jane Conroy, in her riding habit, no less! She looks like Hopalong Cassidy before he went on Dr. Atkins's diet!"

"Let's see."

She looked up. She'd been talking to herself. They

never talked to each other anymore. "Never mind," she murmured, returning to the magazine.

The Indian maid, Rubina, entered with more coffee. She had such a quiet, graceful manner about her. He thought of someone pouring tea for him in the thin, utterly pure air of the Himalayas. She looked at him and smiled shyly, and he felt a stirring. But he mustn't look to every woman he knew for the kind of comfort Stella couldn't give him.

For some reason, he thought of Roxanne Monahan. What a piece of work she was, he thought—tough, hostile, ready to condemn him before she even knew what he was. And yet, sitting here now, it felt good somehow to think of her. Her red hair and her blazing blue eyes were fresh and clean; the woman sitting across from him felt unclean and definitely not of the first freshness. His father and his sister had counseled prudence when he married her, wanting to run a check on her. But he'd been livid about it. One reason he was marrying her was to finally get away from that safe cocoon of David and Merry. Not that he didn't love them—of course he loved them—but he had always felt that the exclusive Broad club to which he belonged, and to which no one else could belong, could be a stifling fraternity. When Stella came along, she was exciting and different and even a little dangerous. He just didn't know *how* dangerous. Now he had to find a solution—an antidote—and it wouldn't be easy.

"What are you staring at?" Stella demanded.

"Nothing."

He rose. "I'll see you tonight for the Governor's dinner?" he asked.

She nodded, bored. They still made "official" appearances together, after which they drifted apart, each to their own room. They hadn't slept together for months and months.

He drained his coffee cup and threw his napkin down on the chair. Taking his private elevator, he went down one floor to his office. He should have had a pole put in, he thought—a good old-fashioned firehouse pole. He was always the first one in. He spent the next hour going over some contracts from the lawyer, yesterday's dictation, some overseas calls which he was perfectly happy to place himself. He didn't like to think of himself as the sort of executive who was above everything. He considered himself an entrepreneur and a maverick who could play by his own rules rather than by those of the gray flannel business world.

After he had been immersed in his work for an hour or so, in walked Lotte with his fresh-squeezed grapefruit juice, hot coffee, and the morning mail.

"You had a good night, Jonathan?" she asked.

"Fine, Lotte. How about you?"

"Me? I haven't slept through a night since my last summer in the Catskills twenty years ago. But," she said, staring at him through her thick glasses, "we're talking about you. Did *you* have a good night?"

What was she driving at? "Yes. I said I did. What's up?"

"I'm glad you had a good night," she said in her nasal voice that could cut diamonds, "because you're gonna have a rotten day, booby." She held up a magazine, its cover facing in. "Are you ready for this?"

His face tightened. "Show me."

"I hate to be the bearer of ill tidings," she went on, "but . . ."

"Show me," he repeated.

It was *New York*. And there was an alarming caricature of him as a sort of behemoth, wild-eyed, straddling a big apple as terrified citizens streamed out like ants, their belongings on their backs. BROADSIDE AT THE CITY! the headline screamed.

"I told you it wasn't gonna be a good day."

"That bastard Frank Loomis," he said. "He won't get off my back. And look at this—they make me look like Attila the Hun."

She peered at it. "I don't know. You look kind of cute to me."

He glared at her. Turning to the article, he read the first paragraph aloud. "'To many elements of the city's population, no name since Son of Sam has struck fear into native hearts as has Jonathan Broad's.'"

"What's with this guy?" Lotte said. "You didn't invite him to your last party or what?"

"'Grabbing up slices of the city under a network of cover operations, the Broad Empire is turning Manhattan into one man's—or, as one unnamed Broad Company employee puts it, "one overgrown boy's"— playground. For a city that thought it had a lot to deal with when Donald Trump came along, Jonathan Broad makes Trump look like a conservative town burgher.'"

"Ouch," said Lotte.

"That son of a bitch," shouted Jonathan. He threw the magazine against the far wall. "Goddamn hatchet job."

"Hey, watch my walls," Lotte said. "I just had 'em painted. Antique eggshell."

"Screw the walls!"

"What's with you anyway?" she said. "Anyone in the public eye's gonna have some bad publicity. It's not like you to take it so seriously."

He looked up at her but said nothing.

"You're too young for a midlife crisis and too old for a tantrum. What gives? Something personal going on?"

Again, he stared at her. "Maybe," he allowed.

She nodded. "Listen to me, Jonathan. I may be nothing much to look at and no great shakes in the wardrobe department, but I know a thing or two. One thing I know is that when you make a mistake, you don't have to live with it all your life. I got rid of my first husband, Lou Gaskin, who sold all our furniture out from under me to underwrite his Aqueduct excursions, and it wasn't easy. But at least it freed me up for Max, God rest his soul."

"OK, Lotte . . ."

"Let me finish," she said firmly. "You are a young man. Granted, you've done more in your life than two average eighty-year-olds put together, but you have to keep in mind that you still are a young man . . ."

"And getting older every minute," he muttered.

"And you've got to weigh your options," she said, ignoring his interruption. "You know, you can build the biggest buildings in New York, the biggest buildings in the world. You can be the best and the smartest and the most powerful. But don't be too great to admit you made a mistake and to do something about it."

The unsaid name hung in the air. All the Broad

Company employees hated Stella, and they had reason to. Because she had climbed out of their social stratum, she had no use for them, and she didn't want them to remind her of what she had been. She was a queen now, and she would lord it over them.

"Capiche?" she said.

He looked at her and grinned fondly. "Shut up and get me some more coffee, will you?" he said.

Stella stood in the lobby of Le Printemps Hotel and looked like she was going to explode. At her side stood society's darling, Jamie Butler, interior designer to the rich and famous, who was asking himself why he had subjected himself to this job and this bitch. The answer, of course, always came back to money. The Broads were scattering it around like birdseed, and now that money was tight, he wasn't about to turn his nose up at a couple of big spenders.

"Look at this yellow!" Stella cried. "I wanted something muted, understated, elegant. This looks like a cheap tearoom!"

You should know from cheap, Jamie thought to himself. It wasn't long since you probably waited tables in just such a place. "You approved the color, Stella."

"Don't give me that shit!" she said furiously. "I don't know what the hell I approved but it certainly wasn't this pukey color. No way in a thousand years I'd approve this kind of junk."

The bitch, he thought, the fishwife. "Well, we can have it corrected," he said with forced equanimity.

She gave him a fierce look. *"You* can have it corrected. And I mean yesterday."

"You certainly don't think that my firm is going to bear the responsibility for . . ."

"You bet your ass I do," she said, hands on supple hips. "You screwed it up, you bought it."

Nervously, he withdrew a silk paisley handkerchief from his jacket pocket and mopped his brow. "I really don't think it's seemly for us to quibble over a few thousand . . ."

"Oh, you don't, do you?" she said, with a sneer. "Let me tell you something. The Broad Company hasn't gotten where it is by being bilked of a few hundred, let alone a few thousand, by anyone. Now fix it, Jamie. Understand?"

He stared at her for a long moment, speechless. Then he nodded, his oversized head bobbing up and down, and spun on his heel, leaving her in the lobby.

She sat down in one of the reproduction Louis Quinze chairs and pulled out a cigarette. She was particularly high-strung, she realized, mostly because of her date later on today with Jerry Castriata, in the goddamn Bronx Zoo, of all places. The other part of it was being here, in the lobby of Le Printemps. She always found it mildly depressing. This is where she and Jonathan had found each other. And look what had become of that. Of course, facing up to it, she hadn't gone into the relationship with a whole lot of expectations. It wasn't as if this were going to be her vine-covered cottage fantasy with four bouncing babies. That wasn't what she was looking for. She was looking for money—francs, marks, yen, she didn't care—but, moreover, she was looking for position. Now she had the money and the position and she was looking for something else, something that Jonathan couldn't provide her. She was looking to make her own mark on the world.

Taking another drag off the cigarette, she wished she had never had the kind of past that included being a reservations clerk at Le Printemps. She wished she had never been a restaurant hostess or a waitress or a model or . . . or any of the other things she'd done when she was on her own. She wished she were like the other women—some of whom she had lunch with in the fancy restaurants as if she were the same as they were—but they'd been born into it; she'd had to beg, borrow, and steal her way in.

She noticed the concierge looking at her. What the hell did he want? He was such a snooty queer, with his "continental" training. Swiss Miss, she called him behind his back. She realized he loathed her, but he was also afraid of her. She took another long drag, held it in her lungs, liked it there, and looked for an ashtray. She had gotten great big beautiful expensive marble ashtrays for all of her hotel lobbies and she couldn't find a goddamn one right now when she needed it.

"Ashtray!" she called, holding up her cigarette.

The concierge sent over a bellboy with a little glass ashtray that had the Le Printemps logo embossed on it.

"What's this?" she demanded.

"An ashtray, madame," said the bellboy, who looked like he was about twelve.

"These aren't the ashtrays I stipulated for this lobby," she said furiously. "Where are the marble ashtrays?"

"I'm . . . uh, I think they were . . . uh, stolen, madame," the flushed bellboy managed.

"Stolen?" She laughed. "That's great. That's just great! I pay security a bundle and a half and they can't even keep people from lugging huge marble ashtrays out of the place underneath their noses!"

She stood and jabbed the cigarette out in the ashtray, as the bellboy held it. "You'd all better get your act together," she said, loud enough for the concierge to hear. "I'm through with carrying dead weight in this operation." She gathered her lynx coat around her, turned, and headed out to her waiting car.

The car turned into the West Gate parking lot of the zoo. Yokimo, her Korean driver, was unsure about where to go, but they followed signs to the fountain and then she got out, told him to wait at the bottom of the stairs, and climbed up the flight which let out at the seal pool.

As she pulled the twenty-thousand dollar coat she'd bought herself for her birthday around her, she looked at the seals playing in their little world, and at the mothers with children, laughing and taking pictures. Clearly a nice thing to do on a day like today, she thought. Take the kid to the zoo. Very nice. So why was she so uninterested, so fundamentally uninterested in all that?

Basically, she didn't like creatures pawing at her for attention, demanding that their needs be met. She cared first of all about her own needs. If that made her a terrible person, then so be it.

Jonathan wanted a child so much. She accused him of wanting to give his father a grandchild—that sexless sister of his seemed unlikely to do so—but maybe he just had more tenderness than she did. Whatever tenderness she'd been born with died very young. And one of the reasons she was seeing to it that their marriage fell apart was just so she wouldn't have to have a child.

She walked down the main promenade in this old, original section of the zoo. There were big, hulking birds of prey in the outdoor cages, and they smelled to her vaguely of decay. She began to get a very tight, crampy feeling deep in her stomach, and she felt suddenly sweaty in her knits. A sign over one of the big old Victorian structures said "Monkey House." She struggled to get a deep breath as she pushed open the door.

On a Tuesday afternoon, the Monkey House was not exactly one of the big draws in town. It also stank. She reached into her bag, pulled out a small atomizer of Chanel eau de cologne, and sprayed it around, trying to fight the simian odor.

"What's the matter, Stella? You don't like nature?" a voice called.

In the dim light, she could make out a figure at the other end of the hall, a fat figure. When he got closer, she could see he had a mouth filled with Cracker Jacks and a bag over his shoulders. "How you been, Stel?" he said. "Good to see you."

"Yeah," she muttered. "Great."

"Hey, now," he said. "You're gonna take that attitude, this is gonna be extra hard on both of us."

She drew out a cigarette and lit it. "Get stuffed," she said, leaning back against the bars of a cage. Just then, there was a horrible snarling sound and she jumped. Looking in back of her, she saw a baboon shaking the bars, furious.

"What the hell's the matter?" she said nervously.

Jerry laughed. "He doesn't like your cigarette. And

he's probably not too wild about your lynx coat either. Not many people in the world would have the balls to wear their fur to the zoo, but you haven't changed a bit, kid."

She ground her cigarette out with her heel. "Listen, Jerry. There's nothing I'd like better than to take a stroll down memory lane with you in the monkey house. But why don't we get down to business, OK?"

"Stella Nevins Broad," he said admiringly. "All business. Except that one night. You really loosened up that night, Stella."

She felt the hairs on the back of her neck prickle. "I don't know what you're talking about," she said, stalling for time.

"Let me refresh your memory," he said. "Cracker Jack?" he offered. She recoiled. "1978. I had the loft down on 25th Street. You came to me through Abby Goshin. Remember Abby?"

"Yeah," she said sullenly. "I remember Abby."

"Got a .22 shot through the keppie down in Miami."

She felt the tightening increase in her stomach. "Why didn't you contact me sooner?" she demanded. "Your type—it would seem you'd be there as soon as you could."

"Let's not talk about 'my type,' Queenie, OK?" he said, losing his smile, but with a Cracker Jack hanging incongruously from his lower lip. "The reason I never surfaced before this, babe, is because I thought I'd lost the negatives. But I didn't. A couple of weeks ago I'm cleaning out an old cabinet and, lo and behold, what do I find? You guessed it. Stella Nevins doing the old mambo with . . ."

"Shut up!" she screamed. The scream resounded

through the hall and the monkeys imitated it, threw it back in her face.

"Nothing to be ashamed of, Stel," he said quietly. "You had a great body. Still do, babe."

She watched him as he took the bag off his shoulder and unzipped it. Her stomach tightened still another notch and her heart pounded thunderously. He took out a black portfolio, unzipped that, looked at her for a moment, and then turned around the portfolio so she could see the goods.

Trying to force herself not to tremble, she took the portfolio from him. There she was. There were her breasts. There was her ass, her vagina. She was showing all of it, and she was smiling for him as she did so. She turned the plastic-coated page. There, on the next page, was another picture, with the Filipina woman. They were entwined with each other, their heads buried in . . .

She threw the book away from her as if it were burning hot. It fell to the floor with a crash that caused the monkeys to stir nervously. "You bastard!" she spat. "You goddamn low stinking pig scum!"

"Take it easy, babe . . ."

"I got a lousy two hundred bucks for that job. A goddamn lousy two hundred bucks and that's it! And now you're coming back to haunt me like some kind of rotten ghoul . . ."

"It's the way of the world, Stella," he said firmly.

"I'd like to watch these apes drink your blood and rip your guts out," she said, her eyes flashing.

"Calm yourself down, baby. I'll give you a day to think about it," he said. "To collect your thoughts, so to speak."

"What do you want?" she cried, finding herself

pleading with him, to her horror. "Tell me what you want!"

He looked at her as if surprised, then laughed. "I want money, babe. What do you think?"

He put the portfolio back in the bag, zipped it up, and headed toward the exit. "Tomorrow," he said. "I'll call you at noon." And then he was out the door.

"Bastard!" she screamed. "You'll be sorry!"

But her words were lost in the imitative screams of the monkeys, watching the humans put on their show.

6

JONATHAN SAT IN the all-white dining room of Milady's, the exquisite new restaurant on the 32nd floor of the Broad Palace. His guest was Daniel Potter, the deputy mayor of finance and economic development. Potter, a short, intense man in his mid-forties, was busily slurping the chanterelle bisque that Jonathan had asked Marcel, the Swiss chef, to prepare especially for them. Potter, who liked to talk about his formative years in Bensonhurst and his early days pushing pencils at Price, Waterhouse and taking the F train home at two in the morning, had never learned a lot about table manners. He possessed what etiquette writers derisively call an "educated thumb," pushing the last of the savory mushroom morsels onto his spoon. But, for all of this, Jonathan needed his help and so looked the other way.

"Now that's a soup," Potter said approvingly, pushing the empty bowl away. "My own mother couldn't have made better."

"Don't let her hear you say that," Jonathan joked, picking at his *salade de fruits de mer*. He never really had much of an appetite for lunch, but most days lunch was unavoidable. He liked nothing better than those days when he could grab a swiss cheese sandwich at his desk.

"Ah, she was a lousy cook," Potter said. "Great woman, lousy cook. She'd take a steak . . . by the time she was through you'd never be able to tell it had come from a live animal."

When the waiter had removed their plates, Jonathan brought up business. "Have you had a chance to look over my proposals?"

Potter nodded. He was blunt and powerful and had made a name for himself managing the mayor's campaign. There were few people in this town thought to be shrewder. "Biting off a big one this time, aren't you, Jonathan?"

"Dan, the city needs this. The waterfront is a mess. We can turn it into a showpiece. River Park will link up with the Convention Center and we'll have something that will make the whole area come alive."

Potter shook his head. "I don't know, Jonathan. We got burned pretty bad on Westway . . ."

"Look at the way Westway was handled, Dan," said Jonathan. "It was thrown like a gauntlet into the faces of the West Siders. I'm willing to offer good cash settlements to all those people in those crumbling old dives. This is going to be the best thing that ever happened to them. I'm going to be Robin Hood."

Potter laughed. "You almost have me believing you," he said, shaking his head.

Jonathan laughed along with him. "OK, OK. I know it's not going to be easy. But it's worth a try, isn't it? And think of what these new buildings will mean to the city. Hundreds of millions of additional dollars in taxes! Do you realize, Dan, what that increase in the city's tax base will mean? More police, better schools, clean subways!"

Potter gave him a wry look. "Jonathan," he said, "you seemed less than interested in increasing the city's tax base when you went after the tax abatement on this lovely Palace here."

"The Palace couldn't handle the kind of tax crunch you folks were pushing," Jonathan said. "River Park can. River Park should."

Potter frowned. "I don't know," he said. "I've always thought in my gut that the waterfront should be left to the sailors, the rats, and the mobsters."

The waiter returned with their main course. Jonathan had broiled pompano, Potter the cassoulet, rich with duck fat. At that rate, Jonathan thought, there would be no more Daniel Potter in a few years' time. "Mmmnh," said Potter, his mouth full, "this is some kind of baked beans, all right."

"Listen, Dan," Jonathan said, "you don't really mean that about the waterfront. It's such a great resource for this city."

"You sound real passionate about it, Jonathan. That's good. But you know, I got this memo from the deputy commissioner of the waterfront. Roxy Monahan. You met with her, right?"

"Right," Jonathan said, not wanting to give more than he had to.

"She seems to think it's a pretty lousy idea. Says the waterfront shouldn't be given over to special interest groups. Assails the idea of entrenched historic neighborhoods making way for ice-cream shops and . . ."

"I'm sick of hearing about ice cream shops!" Jonathan said. "Don't you think I have a sense of love for this city's history? You think I'm really out to turn the whole place into one big shopping mall? I'm talking about renovating wherever and whenever renovation can take place. I'm talking about preservation. Now that doesn't mean I'd want to put a velvet rope around a crumbling old pier, and if that pier does get razed, and commercial space opened up, I don't see what the hell's so wrong with some ice cream on a hot day. But, at base, I see this as a rescue mission for the waterfront."

Potter stared at him, his fork aloft. "You're pretty damned convincing, Jonathan. I'll see what I can do."

"Thank you, Dan," Jonathan replied. "More wine?"

Jonathan and Potter shook hands at the elevator. Then Potter headed down—sharing an elevator with Cher, who had also lunched at the restaurant, and who looked sensational—while Jonathan shot up one floor to his office. Anderson Kendall and Sidney Farrell were waiting for him.

"How was lunch?" Lotte asked, as she handed him his phone messages.

"Great. I don't know about the food but Potter was in a thumbs-up mood."

Lotte reached up to pinch his cheek, and Jonathan sailed into his office.

"Gentlemen," he greeted them, as he sat down. You couldn't imagine two men so different. Sidney Farrell was short, nervous, bespectacled, Jewish, up from C.C.N.Y. and Columbia Business School. Tall and wry, Anderson Kendall fit the perfect Aryan mold and was a product of Harvard and the Harvard Business School. Sidney Jonathan valued for his fierce loyalty; Anderson for his Swiss-watch mind. Unfortunately, they didn't value each other, and the enmity between them was causing a strain in the office. Jonathan had put Sidney, who was pure New York City, onto the Public Development Corporation (PDC) for their approval. Anderson, who hailed from the upstate town of Cazenovia, was assigned to the UDC—the Urban Development Corporation—which was the state entity.

"I see roadblocking all the way on this," Sidney said, bobbing and jiggling in his chair. He always seemed too small for whatever chair he was sitting in, and his nervousness put an edge on every meeting he was in. "I'm already getting calls from the press, and you can see they've got the daggers out, Jonathan . . ."

"I got a call from Frank Loomis today," Anderson said in his broad-voweled Harvard cadence.

"I hope you're not going to talk to that son of a bitch after the hatchet job he did on Jonathan in *New York* magazine," Sidney cried.

"Isn't it better that I should talk to him, Sid, than that we appear unreachable?" Anderson returned smoothly.

"Still, Andy, you've got to watch out for Loomis," said Jonathan. "He's a real shark." Sidney nodded spasmodically, thinking he'd won that point.

"Anyway," Jonathan said, "I've decided to hire Ethel Connelly for the River Park project. I think we need someone like her."

Ethel was the best public relations person in the real estate field. "Here, here," Anderson said.

"Good idea, Jonathan," Sidney piped in.

The meeting continued for another half-hour or so. Jonathan's mind wandered as Sidney and Anderson made their presentations. As he looked out at the cityscape beneath his window, he felt a strange presentiment of trouble. "Enough, gentlemen," he said suddenly, somberly. They looked at each other, seeing who was to blame, and finding each other innocent, they merely got up and left. As they exited, Lotte appeared to announce that Jonathan's sister, Merry, was on her way up.

"Good," said Jonathan. "Send her in, Lotte. And bring me a brownie, will you?" He loved the dark, fudgy brownies from William Greenberg, Jr. and because he hadn't gained a pound since college he saw no reason why he shouldn't allow himself one every now and then. When Merry arrived, he offered her one, but she was obsessive about her weight and asked only for a Perrier.

"You should eat a little, darling," Lotte said. "Put some roses in your cheek."

Merry shook her head. "Please, Lotte. Don't Jewish mother me."

Jonathan watched as Merry pulled off her gloves. She was very well dressed and her hair was beautifully done, but she wasn't what you would call a beautiful woman. She was too thin, too pale, and lacked the kind of animation that beautiful women give off.

They were only sixteen months apart. Throughout their childhood they'd looked alike, Tweedle Dum and Tweedle Dee, but as they grew, Jonathan became brighter and Merry faded, almost as if she had to in order to feed his brightness. For that, Jonathan felt guilty and confused. She had a couple of close girlfriends, but she didn't go out very much with men, never had, and seemed to like quiet evenings to herself best. Jonathan never understood that aspect of her very well, having always liked to be at the center of things.

Just about the only thing she showed any real degree of animation over was design. She had an eye for it. Not just chintz and Hepplewhite chairs, but also the beauty in the line of a teapot, the elegance of a certain kind of simple functional soap dish, the contours of rough brick. She was, consequently, very good at her work, and could have started a considerable business of her own. But she was content to remain in the Broad orbit, as a minor if valuable constellation.

"I brought along some samples of the tile I'd like to use in the lobby at 515 Broadway," she said, reaching into her commodious bag. She brought out two honey-colored tiles, which glinted radiantly in the light streaming through the floor-to-ceiling window.

Jonathan took them in his hand. They were smooth and fine. "Perfect," he pronounced them, "as always. Really, Merry—you've got a great eye."

She looked up at him and smiled, and her face was transformed. It had always been like that—she had always waited for some attention from him.

"Sometimes I think you don't even know how good you are," he said.

"I'm not *that* good," she demurred.

"Don't say that, Merry!" he said angrily. "You're always putting yourself down." He reached out and tenderly touched her cheek. "You're my sister. Don't put my sister down."

She touched the hand that was touching her cheek. "You're sweet, Jonathan."

There was a silence. Signs of affection between them were never expressed that easily. She was too hungry for them, and it made him uncomfortable. "Listen," he said, "I'm on my way over to Montague's to think about what we're going to do with the Buttonhole Bar. Want to come?"

She shook her head. "You know I don't set foot in the hotels, Jonathan. That's Stella's bailiwick."

"Don't worry about Stella," he said. "I'd like your feedback."

"It's easy for you to say, Jonathan. But no," she said, shaking her head. "I'm not setting myself up for that. Frankly, I don't want to tangle with your wife." Merry's antipathy hung in the air like a dark curtain. They both knew that things had progressed beyond the point where Jonathan would defend her. "Why did you do it, Jonathan?" she said bluntly.

"Merry, please . . ."

"Why did you marry her?"

"Don't you think that's my business?" he said.

"No. Not when you bring a woman like that into our family. She's an animal. She's nothing but a . . ."

"I don't want to hear it, Merry," he said.

"Why don't you end it, Jonathan? Cut your losses? Everybody's waiting."

He stared at his sister. "Because she'll skin me alive."

"Don't worry about it," Merry said. "I'll be there with the Band-aids."

"Band-aids aren't going to do the job, sister. She's going to use a jumbo-size machete."

"You sound afraid of her," she said.

He looked away, reached out to touch the honey-colored tiles.

She rose and went to sit next to him on the camel leather sofa. "It's all right to be afraid, Jonathan.

Look at me," she said, in a facetiously bright tone. "I'm afraid all the time."

Jonathan ran a hand through his hair. "I need time, Merry. I know I've made a mistake—a very large mistake—but I need time to figure out a solution."

"There's only one solution."

Just then there was a knock on the door. Lotte, looking unusually serious and subdued, entered. "There's a phone call for you on two, Jonathan," she said, "an important one." The room seemed suddenly to reverberate with a frisson of unease. The siblings looked at each other for an instant, and then Jonathan picked up the phone. "Hello?" he said.

Merry watched him as his face changed, the blood draining from it, the facial bones drawing tight. "What is it, Jonathan?" she demanded.

"When did it happen?" he asked into the phone. "OK, OK. I'll be right there. And," he said, before he hung up, "I want the best possible care, do you understand?"

He hung up the phone. Merry stared at him.

"It's Pop," he whispered.

"He's had a heart attack," she said hollowly.

"He's collapsed," Jonathan said.

"Oh, Jonathan," she moaned.

Suddenly he felt filled with renewed purpose. "Come, Merry," he said, rising and reaching for her hand.

The sight of David Broad on the spare white bed, tubes in his nose, his skin parchment white, tore through Jonathan like a poisoned arrow. This was his father, the man who had always been there for him, the man who had cheered him every step of the way.

89

This man, who already looked like a ghost, could not be leaving him, not now.

"I can't believe it," Merry said, sniffling into a handkerchief. "I just saw him this morning. He looked fine."

"No, he didn't," Jonathan said grimly. "He hasn't looked fine for weeks. We just wanted to believe otherwise."

Dr. Korsmeyer saw them within the hour. More tests were being run on David Broad, but it appeared that renal disease was the culprit. "He's a very sick man," said the eminent internist.

"Will he pull through?" Merry asked.

"There's no telling yet," Dr. Korsmeyer said.

Jonathan and Merry kept a vigil by David's bedside. Jonathan sat there, holding his father's cold hand, wanting to transfer some of his own boundless energy to the man he loved so much. "I can't imagine life without him," he murmured.

"We survived Mommy's death," Merry whispered. "We have each other."

"I don't want him to die," Jonathan anguished. "I need him."

"Oh, Jonathan," said Merry, touching his thick dark hair.

Jonathan jumped up from the bedside and paced the room. "I want everything for him! I want every specialist, every drug that might help him . . ."

"Jonathan, darling," she said, looking up at him with tears in her eyes for her brother's pain. "This is one time that all our money won't buy us what we want. It's in God's hands."

7

"OH, YEAH. OH, baby. Oh, yeah."

She had him wrapped around her little finger, eating out of her hand. She rode him up and down, moving in the little ways that she knew would drive him crazy.

"Oh, Stella, honey . . ."

"Tell me how you like it, Waynie. Tell me how you like it," she crooned in her throatiest tones.

"Any way you do it, honey. Any way," he moaned.

They went together like that, building, building, and then he exploded and she joined him, screeching like a cat in heat, thrashing on top of him and then collapsing at his side.

Moments later, she listened to him snore. She reached in her bag for a smoke, lay back, and looked at the ceiling. She had faked it. Not that he would ever know—she was a hell of a good actress—but, nevertheless, she had faked it. There was a lot on her mind these days; for now, anyway, she'd have to forget about the kind of release she could get from the loving Wayne Mullins gave her. These days she got her release instead from a fine brew of uppers, downers, and pure white snow. Her supplier—the boyfriend of her hairdresser—had the best nose in the business, of that she was sure.

She looked at Wayne, sleeping. She liked him. He was a devil and he played the right cards. But she couldn't tell him about her problems. *The* problem, the Fat Jerry problem.

It wouldn't go away. If she closed her eyes, it stared at her, behind her eyelids, like a phantom. It stalked her dreams and she'd wake up, her antique silk teddies in a sweat. He was ruining her perfect life, Fat Jerry was, and she wanted him scared away.

She thought of asking Wayne about it, but what could be gained from it? It was one thing for her to act less than respectably in the bedroom with him, but for him to know that she had a . . . a past was less than advisable.

She went into the bathroom, washed away traces of his come, dabbed on some Chanel, and put on her clothes. With a groan, he stirred, and she saw him reach out for her. "Stella?" he said foggily.

"Here, babe," she murmured.

"What are you doing all dressed? What happened to Act Two?"

"Hell, Wayne. Don't you ever have anything on your mind but the old in-and-out?" she said, not quite able to suppress her annoyance.

"Sure, honey. Sometimes I think about cracked crab claws. And sometimes I think about CBS or Columbia and which one is most vulnerable to take-over."

She snickered. "A real Renaissance man."

"What got into you?"

"You did," she shot back. "How soon we forget."

"Hey, Stella. Come back to bed."

"I've got things to do, pardner. Give me a break, will you?"

"Tomorrow, hon?"

"I'll call you," she said, stepping out onto the deck of the *Pickle* and trying not to feel the sadness that had invaded her like an ill wind.

She put on her most sincere smile. "Of course every guest we have at the Broad Hotels is treated like a member of the family. That's why we have hot coffee always available in the rooms, and fruit baskets for each guest, and two extra-large bath towels for each individual, and all the other niceties of a home away from home. We won't be outdone by the Helmsleys."

The moderator of the interview show, a bespectacled and preppyish TV personality named Donovan Mead, smiled encouragingly. "Word has it that you're a pretty tough lady to work for, Stella. What do you have to say about that?"

What do I have to say about that? *Heads will roll* is what I have to say about that. Again she smiled, and licked her lips decorously. "Well, Donovan," she said ingenuously, "I think that any person who demands a *standard* of excellence is inevitably going to be met with a certain amount of resentment. But I put forth my record as a minority employer and as a believer in profit-sharing for all."

The fact that there was profit-sharing for none in the Broad Hotels enterprise didn't matter. Who was going to check her facts during the duration of this interview? Later they could call her a bullshitter.

Donovan Mead smiled again and turned to the audience. "We have been talking this hour with the

93

lovely and articulate Stella Broad, director of Broad Hotels, a division of The Broad Company. Thank you, Stella, for sharing your thoughts with us."

She smiled her polite, her sincere, her incandescent, her acutely programmed smile during the smattering of applause, froze it for a moment and then let it melt when the thing was done.

"You were good," Donovan Mead said to her.

"Thanks. A bunch," she said, pulling on her lynx coat.

"I hope you didn't mind some of my tougher questions . . ."

She looked at him. Little closet wimp. "I can take anything you can dish out," she said, turning and walking briskly from the studio.

She got in her car and reached into the bar for the Jack Daniels. She drew the black curtains, sat back, and closed her eyes. This was her little daily bit of heaven. She loved having a car to chauffeur her around. When she had first come to New York— seventeen years old, green as a dollar bill—she'd had to ride the subways. God, how she hated them. Smelly holes in the ground. And greasy guys—and some not so greasy ones, in their gray flannel suits—pushing their cocks against you in the crowd. Once, when she was really low, really hungry, she started the thing. She stood in front of a man dressed impeccably in a blue flannel suit, reading the *Wall Street Journal*. As the car got more and more crowded with each stop, she got closer and closer to him. Soon her buttocks were up against him, and he wasn't reading so carefully, and a stop or two later she began to grind up against him, feeling him get hard. When she got out at her stop, he got out with her. There was no coyness. She invited him up to her place, she did what she had to do, and he left a hundred dollar bill on the bureau.

She did that sort of thing now and then. She'd swear on a stack of Bibles that she hadn't ever been a prostitute, but she let herself take things from men. Why not? Why the hell not? Men took from her. She hated people who thought things came for free, these rich New York women with their blond hair and their expensive silks and tweeds. They'd never known what it was like to be five years old, standing outside in a concrete yard littered with broken bottles and scattered with stinkweed, your mother braying at you. *Stella Nevins! You come in here, miss! You come in here or I'll give you a licking like you never got before, little stuck-up miss!* And then the years in high school, trying to make good, trying to be as pretty and popular and capable and respected as the "good girls" from the "good neighborhood." But every night, when the "good girls" were going for ice cream sodas with their Chip or Skipper or Rusty, she was giving head to her stepfather in the living room while her mother snored in the bedroom.

She was so, so angry. Jonathan, when they'd been married for a while and he had realized the depth of her anger, told her he wanted to help. She wouldn't let him in, though. If she told him her secrets, he'd be finished with her. He'd sent her to a psychiatrist on Central Park West. An office like a football field, everything leather and brass, like something out of Sherlock Holmes.

—Why do you seem so angry, Mrs. Broad?

—I'm not angry!

—Listen to yourself.

—I don't need to listen to myself at a hundred bucks an hour.

She didn't need that kind of therapy. She needed this kind of therapy. She needed a big plush car, with black curtains to keep eyes away and a bar with prime liquor, and a television and a stereo and a man to wait for her, the motor running, as she shopped at Bendel's and Lina Lee's. She needed it because the world was trying to close in on her. She wouldn't let Jerry Castriata have any money. It was her money and she wasn't going to share it.

The car pulled up to the Palace and the doorman—Eddie, with a few tied on from lunch at the Bantry Grill and his nose shining red as an exit sign—opened the car door for her.

"Hi, Eddie," she said.

"Hi, Mrs. Broad," he fawned, touching the brim of his cap. He loved her. She gave him not only money at Christmas but a bottle of twelve-year-old Scotch. He'd do anything for her, Eddie would, she mused, as she headed through the lobby of deep rose-colored marble.

Back in the apartment, she had Rubina draw a bath. It was nice having an Indian maid, she thought, as she threw her clothes into a heap on the floor and stepped into the bathroom; they throw rose petals into the bathwater. Sinking down into the water, she closed her eyes, and allowed her senses to be filled with the luxury of her life. She wouldn't let anyone endanger this.

With a sudden clarity, she sat up in the bath. She practically jumped from the tub, wrapped one of the huge white Porthault bath sheets around her, and picked up the phone. She was amazed that she still remembered the number—a private number, unlisted, unattainable. 516-333-3323. She waited a moment as the phone rang. Then someone picked it up.

"Good afternoon," said the voice, slightly foreign but with a well-bred tone.

"Good afternoon," she said, trying to keep her voice under control. "May I speak with Gabriel Messina," she said.

There was the briefest of pauses. "Whom may I say is calling?"

She thought a moment. "Stella Nevins," she decided to say, fighting down the feeling that she was returning to a former life.

It wasn't safe to have the chauffeur drive her out to Kings Point, so she took the plum-colored Lamborghini that she kept for her personal needs. As she drove, she kept glancing at herself in the side-view mirror. Did she see the beginnings of a clogged pore? She had a tendency toward broken-out skin when she was under this kind of stress. She'd have to schedule a session for tomorrow with Olga, who'd whip her skin into shape with her special formula of birch bark extract and crushed almonds.

But at least she knew her clothes were right. She was wearing Valentino burgundy leather pants that had cost a cool grand. High black leather boots, Ralph Lauren. A white Krizia silk shirt. No bra. Black pearls. The lynx coat.

She hadn't seen Gabriel in six years. They had a real history together. He had picked her up when she was a hostess at a now defunct Manhattan nightclub called Pierrot's. It was an elegant place, and she had no reason to feel anything less than gratified to have the job. She didn't have to show any skin; she didn't have to grease any palms; and, unlike some other joints she had worked in, nobody tried to slip a hand underneath her skirt. Gabriel Messina, then in his forties, with an incredible head of silver-gray hair, classic features that would have qualified him to be a silent-screen matinee idol, and a lithe, strong body encased in five-hundred dollar Italian suits, was a regular. He liked her from the first—he'd flash his golden dimples at her and slip her a hundred here and there, which for him was like bus fare—and in time he asked her to join him for dinner. Did she think about it too long? Fat chance. She'd been living on Spam then, sliced cold on white bread, grilled with pine-apple spears.

He was good to her, Gabriel was. He showered gifts on her, and took her places. London for a weekend, Rome for three days, Bimini every weekend in January. And he didn't just take from her in bed; he gave too. But he was wildly possessive. If he didn't know where she was every moment of the day, he'd go into a rage. And, too, he had certain . . . kinks. He was very into masquerade. He had her dress up as a bride once, and once as a stewardess. He had a lot of costumes on hand. Once he made her dress up as a little girl, and he wanted her to call him Daddy. She wouldn't do it, it struck too close to home. And he screamed at her, bellowed at her, even struck her, because she was an ungrateful bitch.

She pulled away. For a while, she got threatening phone calls, and worried what kind of revenge—real Sicilian revenge—he would exact. But then he stopped and she went back to her life, first modeling on the Avenue and then the job as reservations clerk at Le Printemps. And the rest, as they say, was history.

She got off the parkway and drove down Northern Boulevard. Amazing how clearly she knew where she was going. The streets became wider, greener, more polished, more perfect. Here and there were flashes of the glittering blue water of the Sound. A perfect peaceful enclave, she thought, as she approached Gabriel's estate, so incongruously built on a river of blood.

At the wrought-iron gates she announced herself over the intercom and was admitted. She drove the startling green expanse of lawn up to the front door of the enormous Tudor mansion. The grounds were exquisitely kept and here and there she saw people dart in and among the bushes—the gardeners as field animals.

The butler opened the front door. He was dark-complexioned, perhaps Indian or Indonesian, reed-slim, and pleasantly toothy. "Madame?" he said.

"I'm . . . Stella Nevins. Here for Mr. Messina."

"Please," the butler salaamed, admitting her.

The entrance foyer was nothing less than baronial. There were mounted game animals on the walls—she suddenly remembered that Gabriel enjoyed hunting —and much stained glass and dark wood. The butler led her into the library, where Gabriel was seated at a large desk, talking on the telephone.

She stood there for a moment, as he talked. He hadn't yet looked up, and she felt chagrined and even humiliated. He hadn't seen her in years and yet he felt impelled to finish his phone conversation. She would have liked, just then, to turn on her heel and get out of there. But then he hung up the phone, looked up at her, smiled brightly, and said, "You haven't changed a bit, Stella."

"Neither have you, Gabriel."

"Bullshit. Look at my eyes. Look at those bags. You think I should have them done?"

"They give your face character, Gabriel," she managed, feeling her heart pounding. "I think you look great."

"Character," he scoffed. "Who the hell needs character? That's a nice way of saying I've got interesting lines in my face. You want to see interesting lines you go look at the Brooklyn Bridge."

She smiled. "Same old Gabriel," she said. "You'll never change."

"But you changed, didn't you, babe?" he said, scrutinizing her. "Top of the world now, huh? Mrs. Jonathan Broad. See you in all the society pages. Don't you go to all those dinners they got at the museum? The ones where Jackie O always hangs out?"

"I don't go to *all* of them, Gabriel. I go to some of them, but not . . ."

"Cut the crap, Stella. You go to all of them. You've become a great lady of New York. But that doesn't explain why you're here, does it?" He got up and walked around to her side of the desk. He was tall and thin still; he'd kept himself in very good shape. She blushed as memories of them together flashed like strobes through her mind.

"Right to business, aren't you?" she said, with a slightly mocking tone.

He reached out and grabbed her arm—grabbed it

100

hard. "So what's the story, Stel? Old home week? Memory Lane? What are you doing here?"

"Stop it. You're hurting me!"

"You hurt me plenty," he said. "Left me holding the bag, didn't you?"

She pulled her arm away and then, glaring at him, rubbed it. "Shall I go?" she suggested.

"No. You just got here," he said. He went to the bookcases, pushed a button, and some leather-bound volumes revolved to expose a neat vest-pocket bar. "Jack Daniels still your drink?" he asked.

"You introduced me to it," she said. "I haven't given it up."

"I sure hope you haven't given up a lot of things I introduced you to," he said. "You were a great student."

"I haven't forgotten any of your lessons, Gabriel."

He brought back her drink and they sat near each other on the scarlet leather sofa. "So tell me, beautiful," he sighed. "What do you need?"

Her eyes grew moist. She was afraid he would think she was acting for him—and the fact was that she didn't need an onion to get the tears going if she needed to—but this time they were legitimate.

"Come on, kid. Cut the waterworks," he said.

She felt stung. The bastard. She wanted to say as much, but she couldn't. It was idiotic to even consider it. "I need your help," she said.

He savored this one, rolling it around on his tongue, and a little smile formed at the corner of his lips. "What could I possibly do for you that the eminent Jonathan Broad, in all his glory, cannot achieve?"

Her hand touched her hair nervously, and she

looked away, toward the pink marble fireplace, where a fire raged so strangely on a warm day. "Someone's been trying to hurt me, Gabriel," she whispered.

He reached out to touch her hair. "Who'd want to hurt you?" he said huskily. "That pretty face."

"A long time ago," she began, "I was very much in need. I was hungry, Gabriel. Really hungry."

"No, no, sweetheart. It pains me to think of you being hungry."

"I was out of a job. It was the Christmas season."

"Hungry at Christmas?" he said, with a remote half-smile. "This is going to be no holds barred, everything but the bloodhounds."

She rose and pulled her coat around her.

"What is it?" he said.

"You're mocking me," she cried. "I won't stand for it. I don't care how much I need help, I won't be made a fool of."

He reached out and seized her wrist. "You always were proud, weren't you? Too damned proud for your own good."

"No," she said, shaking her head. "I wasn't always proud. Once, when I thought I had nothing to lose, I let a man talk me into doing something filthy in front of a camera. I took my clothes off, and put on black lingerie and black leather with holes cut out for the tits and I spread myself for his camera and then he brought out another girl and we went at each other, between each other's legs, our lips and tongues all over, and I didn't care, I didn't give a good goddamn then for that or anything else in the world and now here I am, here, and I . . ."

She stopped herself. She looked at him, then looked away and burst into tears.

"Don't cry, Stella," he said dully. "It doesn't become you."

She stopped almost as soon as she had begun. "You're right. It's not the real me. The real me should tell the world where to get off, but I'm not doing that, Gabriel. I'm beaten."

He stared at her and then shook his head. "Bullshit," he said. "As Casey Stengel once said, 'It's not over 'til it's over.'" He leaned into her. "So what do you need, babe? Tell Papa."

"I need someone scared away, Gabriel," she said, her eyes narrowing. "Jerry Castriata—a fat shlub, whose only claim to fame is the fact that he got me in my birthday suit . . ."

"And playing birthday party games with another woman, huh? That wasn't the smartest thing you ever did."

"All right, Gabriel. I'm smarter now. I know there's nothing for nothing."

There was a silence. "So what do you want me to do?"

She looked at him for a moment and then shook her head. "You've always been good at getting people out of jams . . ."

"I'm good when people pay me to be good, Stella," he said frankly.

"If it's money, Gabriel, it's no problem . . ."

"Don't insult me, sweetie," he said, with a flash of anger that obliterated his dimples and turned his face stark and dangerous. "Does it look like I need your money? Look around. You see beauty? You see gorgeousness? Your little Jonathan Broad with all his buildings, running around the city like a goddamn kid with an erector set . . . I could buy him and sell him,

103

babe, and don't you forget it. So don't come here and start talking money, understand?"

She felt her heart pounding. "Then what do you want?"

"Your other talents, Stella," he said, putting a hand on her knee.

"Gabriel, that's over. That's history . . ."

"Don't jive me," he said contemptuously, his hand moving up her thigh, pressing into her vulva that was encased in the burgundy leather. "I always had a yen for you, Stella. You knew what you were doing. You were some kind of a pro, let me tell you."

She couldn't help but get excited by his words. They had made fireworks together, and to hear him linger over it . . . "Yeah," he went on in that husky voice. "You remember, don't you?"

She felt herself getting wet. This was dangerous . . . and she loved it. Maybe, just maybe, in the back of her mind, or perhaps not that far back, she had thought that this might happen . . .

"You'll help me?" she murmured, as she moved closer to him.

"Oh, baby," he said, reaching into her silk blouse with his big, rough hand. "I'll help you, luv. We'll scratch each other's back."

She met him with her lips and they probed each other for a long time before she pulled away. "Thank you," she said, and he laughed, and she felt safe and thrilled at once.

He stood up and undid his pants. Presenting himself to her, his hands on his hips, he smiled broadly and watched as she went to work. It wasn't the worst work in the world, she thought, as she administered to him. It wasn't digging ditches. It wasn't slinging hash.

It was well paid, too, she thought, as she heard him moan. When he reached for her, pulled her up to her feet, took off her blouse, ripped off her leather pants, she worried about the butler, but he told her the butler knew not to let anyone come in when the door was closed. Then he had her on the couch, the leather couch, and it was cold at first but then warm, and he was on top of her, grunting like a bull as he slammed into her again and again and again, all the while her thinking that it wasn't bad work, not bad work at all, and that she was good at it, and she liked it. She liked being good at it, she thought, as she moved with him, gripped him, flung her legs around him, urging him deeper into her, scratching him, biting him, as he came in a shudder, and she found herself screaming and coming with him too, not faking it now, not faking it, but reveling in it.

She sat on the sofa, looking into the mirror of her compact. The pore was definitely clogged. She might have to change her foundation, she thought—her skin was getting more sensitive as she grew older. Then she felt his hands on her again, as he moved behind her, gripping her breasts and pressing his hardness against her. "I've got to go," she moaned, as he nuzzled her neck.

"Never," he said.

"Don't worry," she said, turning to face him. "I'll be back."

"Don't you ever leave me again."

"How could I leave you?" she said in a little girl voice that she had the sense to use sparingly. "You're making it all better for me."

He kissed her and then pulled her away to stare at

her. "Beautiful," he said appreciatively. "But there's one other thing."

"Oh, Gaby," she said. "I told you I have to go."

"No, babe," he said, with a shadow of a smile. "About our deal. There's one other thing."

She allowed a flicker of confusion to show on her face, as she felt her mouth go dry. "What?"

"I take care of the fat boy as long as you take care of me . . ."

"I know," she said tensely. "Haven't I?"

"Yes, babe, you have," he said. "But, as good a piece of ass as you are, there's more."

Piece of ass. She felt like he had slapped her across the face. She stared at him, watching his visage darken. "What is it, Gabriel?" she said.

"About River Park," he said, reaching into his humidor for a cigar.

She stared at him. "What about River Park?" she said, after a moment.

"I want a piece of it," he replied, running the cigar under his nose, and then sucking on it to wet the tip.

She smiled. "You don't know Jonathan . . ."

"But you do," he said brusquely. "I want the restaurants and I want the saloons. That's the deal."

Now her heart was pounding furiously—horse hooves on a cobblestone street. "That's impossible. Believe me, Jonathan runs a clean ship. Squeaky-clean."

He lit up, thoughtfully took three or four puffs, and watched as the smoke collected on the ceiling. "Really?" he said. "Then how do you figure he got stuck with you?"

"You bastard," she cried, reflexly covering her breasts with her arms.

"That's the deal, babe. Take it or leave it."

"You bastard!"

"You said that already. Listen, I've got to go. Sleep on it, Stella. And let me know."

He stood there, smoking, naked, as she got dressed. There was nothing, she thought, as degrading as having to get dressed in a hurry while someone watched you. As she walked to the door, he called out to her.

"What is it?" she demanded.

He smiled at her sympathetically. "Listen, honey," he said. "Just remember—this too shall pass."

She looked at him, turned, and then slammed the door as hard as she could.

8

JONATHAN WATCHED HIS father sleep. He had come back from the dead . . . but just barely. Now his father was set up in his own home, with around-the-clock nurses, fighting his way back to health. But it was a long road back and his father was tired and irritable and often seemed unwilling to make the trip.

"Now, Mr. Broad," said the Jamaican nurse, "you must be drinking your broth, you hear?"

Jonathan watched as the nurse brought the spoon up to his father's lips again. His father held the broth in his mouth for a moment and then let it dribble out the sides. Jonathan felt his stomach lurch and went out into the library.

"What's the matter?" asked Merry, looking up from her bargello. She was always busy with needlepoint or something.

Jonathan shook his head. "Nothing."

She went back to her work, her face pensive as she stitched. He couldn't help staring at her, wondering what she was all about, sitting here stitching, hour after hour.

"What are you looking at?" she asked, when she became aware of his attention.

"Nothing," he said.

She frowned. She had never liked attention. He realized now, as he watched her with her handwork, that she had always been domestically oriented. She should have had a home with a husband and children and babies to knit for and little girls' dresses to make and cookies to cut. But she didn't, none of it, and he wondered why. Her movements seemed cramped and obsessive. She was knitting a web around herself, around her life, and he couldn't stand to see it.

He stood up. "Time to go."

"So soon?"

He'd been here an hour. Every morning he came by for an hour and then too in the evening. Merry seemed to spend her life here—he couldn't. "I want you to get out today, Merry," he said in very sober tones. "It's not healthy for you to be spending so much time here."

"Oh, please, Jonathan. Don't start sounding like a doctor."

"Merry, you're very devoted. No one could be a better daughter . . ."

"You're right, Jonathan," she said, looking up, fiercely clutching her bargello square. "No one has been a better daughter than Merry Broad."

Her expression was rigid and strained. "Merry, you're under a lot of stress here," he began. "I really think it's best if you let Papa . . ."

"Don't tell me what's best!" she cried. "You're always telling me what's best! You always think you know everything!"

Shocked, he could only stare in a kind of wonder, as if he'd never seen her before. She put a hand up to her mouth and looked away. "Merry," he whispered, touching her shoulder.

She turned to him. "I'm sorry, Jonathan," she said hollowly.

"No, I'm sorry, Merry," he said. "If I thought, all along, you thought that about me, I'd have . . ."

"Don't berate yourself, Johnny," she said, with a gentler tone. "You know very little about what I'm thinking."

He stared at her, realizing that what she said was the truth.

"You're not yourself," Abigail said, as she drew a lazy circle around Jonathan's nipple with her fingernail.

"Really?" he said. "I thought I did OK. At least it sounded like you came off."

She frowned and sat up in bed, reaching for the champagne on the night table. "Don't be vulgar," she said with her Seven Sisters intonation. "That's not what I'm talking about. Obviously, Jonathan Broad would never leave a woman whom he was servicing unsatisfied," she said, a touch of irony, even mockery, in her voice.

He yawned. "So then what exactly are you talking about?"

"I'm talking out of concern, dear, not out of dissatisfaction. You just don't seem yourself."

Her worry touched him. Although she was good fun in bed and out of bed—bright, relatively easy to please, relatively uncomplicated—he had never regarded concern for others as one of her salient characteristics. To know that she cared about the real him, as divorced from his money, his power, and his cock, was a nice thing. He had never really gone to women for that sort of thing, more comfortable in the role of giver, caretaker, provider. That had been the foundation of his relationship with Stella, the beautiful, poor girl on her own in New York City—that and the sex.

"I suppose it's my father," he said finally.

"Poor David," she said, a sympathetic little moue forming on her lovely lips. "Has he taken a turn for the worse?"

"It's pretty much status quo," Jonathan said, "but he's just a shadow of his former self. He was never a dynamo, but he was always . . . solid. Like an oak. Now he's thin, painfully thin, and his color is poor, and he sits in a chair and his eyes look rheumy and sad."

She reached out to touch his cheek. "It's hard," she said. "Have you thought of having him moved to a convalescent home? Perhaps it would be better for everyone if he wasn't still in the apartment."

He stared at her but her face was all sympathy. He would have liked to laugh. This is the way she thought: if something was unpleasant, then you removed it. Or, better yet, you had someone else remove it—the maid, if handy, or the gardener.

"It's something to think about," she said, in her cool, refined voice.

"Yes," he said, nodding heavily. "It's something to think about."

She put her glass down, and reached out to touch him. "Mmmnh," she said with a little smile. *"Encore?"*

He looked at her, her coolly inviting smile, then pressed her back against the sheets. She gave a little gasp as he pushed ruthlessly into her, ground against

111

her and pushed as deep as he could, wanting to impale her. She groaned delightedly, receiving him, not knowing that it was anger at her, at her glibness, at her lack of regard for his father and for human life in general, that made him go at her that way.

When it was over, she sighed a little. "Oh, that was good," she said delightedly, like a fine lady taken to the fights and loving every minute of it. He said nothing as he dressed and went on with his day.

It was on site at 511 Broadway, a huge downtown office complex that the Broad Company was putting up, that Anderson Kendall, looking a little incongruous with a hard hat on his elegant golden hair, first mentioned the name Sherman Maloney. Jonathan would always remember the moment on the outside elevator up to the fortieth floor, and how Sidney Farrell, looking like it was dress-up time with a hard hat on his balding head, tried to undercut Anderson by scoffing at his rival's concerns.

"A tenant in a rooming house on West 23rd and Twelfth Avenue?" Sidney demanded. "About this you're bothering Jonathan?"

"Jonathan," said Anderson, ignoring Sidney, "this man Maloney, he's not just your average New York retiree. He's a one-man media machine. He's already got five reporters down at the building and he's filibustering about what a big bad guy the Broad Company is for wanting to buy him and his neighbors out for the 'paltry' sum of $20,000."

"The ingrate," Sidney fumed. "These people get twenty grand dropped in their laps and they're complaining."

"Get a hold of yourself, Sidney," Jonathan said, as

the three of them stepped out onto the unfinished fortieth floor. Sidney, although around construction most of his adult life, had never gotten fully comfortable with heights and so turned a peculiar shade of pea green. "Sit down, Sidney," Jonathan instructed.

"No, that's okay. I'll just . . ."

"Sit down, Sidney," Jonathan said firmly.

Sidney sat down. The view—the sense of height—was dizzying. Jonathan got a fleeting feeling of pure exhilaration. But then Anderson was back murmuring in his ear, "Jonathan, this Sherman Maloney is like your classic jailhouse lawyer. He used to be a court reporter. Evidently he was married for many years, had no children, his wife got all sorts of cancer and he used up his savings. Ten years ago he moved into this rooming house. All of his neighbors have similar stories. You've got one apartment there with three old deaf men living together, another one that's got a woman of ninety or so with forty cats, it's that kind of thing. And Maloney, who looks kind of like Barry Fitzgerald in *Going My Way,* has this amazing Gaelic gift of gab and is out to save the republic."

"Well, if twenty thousand won't do," said Jonathan, "I guess we'll just have to sweeten the pot."

"I don't know, Jonathan," said Anderson. "This guy doesn't seem to care about the money . . ."

Jonathan looked straight at Kendall. "Everyone cares about the money, Andy. "Don't ever forget that."

"That's right," Sidney chimed in. "And while we're on the subject of malcontents, let me reintroduce the name of one Ms. Roxy Monahan. Evidently at a dinner the other night she cornered the governor and gave him a dish full of badmouthing about River

Park. I don't know what the woman's problem is but she's certainly a noisy one, Jonathan, and I think we'd better address it. Do you want me to take care of it?"

Jonathan thought a moment. "No, Sidney. Leave that to me."

When they got back to the office, Jonathan had Lotte put a call in to Monahan. The better part of an afternoon went by and she hadn't returned the call. Jonathan asked Lotte to call again and this time she picked up.

"Ms. Monahan?"Jonathan said.

"Yes?"

"It's Jonathan Broad."

"Yes. I know. I'm sorry I didn't get a chance to return your call."

"That's all right. I won't take it personally."

There was an awkward pause that he expected her to fill, but she didn't.

"Ms. Monahan, I was wondering if you'd care to join me for lunch tomorrow? I thought we should discuss River Park further. I don't think I was able to fully convey to you my plans."

There was another awkward pause. "Very well," she said, "on one condition."

"What's that?"

"You call me Roxy."

He laughed—thank God she had some sense of humor. "Okay, Roxy. Let me put my secretary on with the details."

Maybe, just maybe, this would work out, he thought. But what surprised him more—and what he couldn't even begin to comprehend—was that he wanted to see her.

* * *

All around him were the rich and the famous. Come hell or high water, Stella usually made lunch at Le Cirque too, and he wondered what she was up to. The thought of her being with someone caused him no pain, no feeling at all. After all, if he had the right to fool around, so did she. And he had the feeling she did—in a big way. Catching sight of the maitre d' leading Roxy Monahan to his table, he rose and greeted her.

"Fancy place," she said, sitting down.

"It's sort of fun," he said, "and the food's good."

"Look at these women," she said, glancing around. "Isn't that Barbara Walters?"

"Yes. She eats here regularly."

"And that's Ivana Trump, isn't it? Wait a minute!" she cried, her fiery red hair framing her face. "That's Richard Nixon."

"So it is," he said, amused.

She turned to him, horrified. "I cannot eat lunch in a restaurant with Richard Nixon sitting fifteen feet away."

Looking at her he saw she was serious. "That's a little extreme, isn't it?"

She frowned. "I hate rich food and the sound of bangling bracelets on rich ladies' wrists and fawning captains who sneer at people in double-knit suits. What can I say? I wasn't brought up that way." She looked at him and blinked. "I hope you don't mind my frankness."

He rose suddenly. "Let's go."

She looked up. "Where?"

"That's for you to decide."

She smiled a little, a crooked sort of smile, and got up. "An emergency, Jean-Paul," he explained to the

115

maitre d', who looked surprised but unflappably deferential.

"Nothing grave, Monsieur, *j'espère,*" said Jean-Paul.

"No, Jean-Paul. My apologies," he said, as he took Roxy's arm and led her out.

In front of the restaurant they grinned at each other. "So where to?" he asked.

"Nedick's?"

"Oh, come on," he said. "Let's not get that elemental."

"You never ate in a Nedick's, did you?" she demanded.

"Come on, Roxy," he said. "I've had an Orange Julius, I've had a Sabrett hot dog, I've had a meatball hero. I wasn't raised in an ivory tower. But I do have an appreciation for the better things in life."

"The better things in life are not necessarily the most expensive ones," she pointed out.

He decided not to address that one. "Where do you usually eat lunch?" he said.

She shrugged. "I don't make it a big deal. I grab a sandwich at my desk. If I'm in an expansive mood with something to celebrate, I go over to Chinatown. Sometimes I go over to my father's boat."

"Your father's boat?" he asked with a quizzical expression.

She looked at him. She realized he didn't know much about her at all, and she couldn't help feeling a little disappointed. After all, she was something of a minor celebrity. *Ms.* and *Savvy* and *Working Woman* had all written her up—"tugboat captain's daughter becomes deputy waterfront commissioner." She guessed he didn't bother to know about anyone but

116

himself. "Yes," she said. "With my brothers my father owns and operates a tugboat, the *Galway Bay.*"

"Aha," he said, with a nod. "So that's why you're so protective of Slip 20 . . . whatever."

"Slip 27," she said firmly. "You really shouldn't be so cavalier about it, Mr. Broad. The lives of certain people depend upon it."

"Hey," he said. "You made a big point of telling me to call you Roxy. So if this lunch is going to go on, you'd better call me Jonathan. Part of this lunch, as far as I see it, is for you to educate me about the lives of those people. So start educating, Roxy, and stop chastizing."

It was funny, she thought. Standing here on the street, Jonathan Broad suddenly seemed like a human being. Not a *Wunderkind,* not a wizard, not a whirlwind. "OK," she said, taking a deep breath. "You want to be educated? Let's start with the *Galway Bay.* Object lesson number one."

"You're kidding," he said with a grin.

"I'm not kidding. We'll grab a couple of tuna sandwiches on board. My father makes a simply divine tuna sandwich," she camped, unable to resist the tease. They got into his Rolls and headed downtown.

"Would you like a drink?" he asked.

She giggled—she couldn't help it. "Don't tell me you've got a bar in this thing."

He stared at her. "You know, Roxy, you don't have to say everything that comes into your mind."

She shrugged. "That's the way we are, we Monahans. I guess it's sort of a problem, but what can I do? Anyway, you've been pretty good about it. At least, you were a good sport about the restaurant."

"I was intrigued," he admitted. "No one had ever told me they found Le Cirque unendurable."

"I don't know about unendurable," she said. "It's just not me."

"People who always want to be themselves don't always get very far," he said.

"Some people don't always want to get very far," she countered.

"You don't strike me as one of those people," he said. "You seem pretty ambitious."

"Up to a point," she agreed. "I'm not willing to compromise myself. As Lillian Hellman said, I'm not cutting my conscience to fit this year's fashion."

He regarded her frankly. "Don't you think you take things a little too seriously?"

"What do you mean? Is that in poor taste or something, to take things seriously?"

He shook his head. "You're really out to cast me as the bogeyman, aren't you? Taking everything I say and turning it around against me."

She shrugged. "I'm a lawyer. I guess I can't help that sort of thing."

"Well, listen, Roxy," said Jonathan, pouring himself a mineral water, "I take things seriously too . . ."

"Like making money?"

"There you go again."

"I'm sorry," she laughed. "I'm a born gadfly. I can't help it."

He considered this for a moment. "I care about a lot of things, like the future of this city and the quality of life here and, yes, making money. Or at least making money work."

"Work for whom?" she challenged.

"Work for everyone."

They looked evenly at each other. "So what are you telling me? That you're this year's Eugene Debs? Spreading the wealth and all that?"

"Gadfly, my ass," he said angrily. "You're just a very hostile woman, that's all. Plain and simple."

"Everything's plain and simple to you, isn't it?" she countered. "Buy, sell. Win, lose."

"If you mean do I believe in myself and what I'm doing, then the answer is yes."

There was a silence in the car. He looked out at the Wall Street crowds and felt furious.

"We can terminate this lunch now if you wish," Roxy said. "It doesn't seem to have gone very well."

"No, it hasn't," he replied. "But I'm hungry, and you've put the taste of tuna fish in my mouth."

"It probably hasn't been there in years," she said drily.

"Last Wednesday. Individual can, with tomato," he shot back.

She looked at him and laughed—she couldn't help it. "You're full of surprises, aren't you?"

"Yes," he said, his eyes gleaming. "Stick around and you'll see."

The car let them off at Peck Slip, where her father usually pulled in to do his lunchtime chores. Roxy sprang out of the car, waving. "Pop!" she called.

Edmund Monahan, nailing down a plank, looked up and his big red face grew even redder with delight. "Roxy!" he cried. "What a surprise."

"Come on," she said to Jonathan, leading him down the pier, briefly considering his custom-made Turnbull & Asser shirt, seven hundred dollar Aquascutum suit, gold Patek Phillipe watch, and

English bootmaker's shoes. In her heart of hearts, she secretly hoped that he would sit down on a mackerel.

"Hi, Pop," she said, as she got on board the *Galway Bay*. "This is Jonathan Broad. Jonathan, this is Edmund Francis Patrick Monahan."

Her father, bless him, wiped his greasy old hand on his coveralls before shaking the gentleman's hand. "Pleased to meet you, sir," Edmund said, evidently forgetting who Jonathan Broad was, and thinking he might be one of Roxy's erstwhile suitors.

"What's this?" burbled Ryan, coming up from below, carrying a gas can. "Roxy with a guy? Eh, Denny," he called to his brother, who was in the galley. "Roxy's got a guy."

She flushed. Sometimes it seemed as though Ryan hadn't changed since he was eight years old. Wait— he'd been considerably cuter when he was eight.

Wiping his hands on a dishtowel, Dennis came out to see, his face full of mischief and his eyes sparkling. "Nice duds," he commented, looking Jonathan over. Jonathan laughed, seeming to enjoy it all immensely, particularly Roxy's discomfiture.

Edmund turned to give Ryan a resounding shove. "Pull yourself together, lad," he hissed. "Mr. . . . Broad, is it? Allow me to introduce my sons, Ryan and Dennis." More handshaking all around, and then Brendan emerged from the hold, immersed in the *New Statesman,* which evidently had kept him busy during his toilet activities. "And my eldest son," said Edmund, "Brendan Monahan. Brendan," said Edmund, "this is Mr. Broad."

Brendan looked up, saw first Jonathan's extended hand, then looked at Jonathan's face, and then scowled. "You're Jonathan Broad, aren't you?" he said.

"Yes," Jonathan replied.

"Well, what are you doing here?"

"Brendan!" Roxy cried. Her brother could be even more blunt and rude than she, and suddenly she was in the position of mollifier, a position she did not enjoy.

"Well," said Jonathan calmly, "I was invited here for a tuna fish sandwich."

"And to see how the other half lives, eh?" said Brendan, with undisguised bitterness. "Is that right, Roxy?"

"Yes, Brendan," Roxy said. "I thought it would be a good idea for Mr. Broad to see how we live."

"Well then," said Edmund, "let's stop all the yammering and get down to lunch, shall we?"

"Pop, can we give Mr. Broad a little taste of the harbor along with his tuna?" Brendan asked.

"Well," said Edmund, "I suppose we can take the old girl out for a little spin if Mr. Broad is interested."

They all looked at Jonathan. "Yes, sir," he said, "very interested."

In a matter of moments they were out on the water again, all the brothers at their stations, the air filled with the sound of tooting, sea horns, the slap of the wind. "Warm enough?" Roxy asked Jonathan.

"Yes, thank you."

"The wool of that suit is so fine," she said. "You'd be better off with a coarser weave in this sort of situation."

"My skin is very sensitive," he said. "If I wear anything coarse, I break out into a rash." She looked

121

at him and he grinned. He was parodying himself—
beating her to it—stealing her fire.

As the *Galway Bay* sailed the New York Harbor,
Roxy observed Jonathan as he sat eating tuna and
listening to Edmund's life story. Much to her surprise
Jonathan proved to be a hell of a good listener,
nodding sympathetically and asking all the right
questions. When Edmund took a breath, Jonathan,
between bites of the tuna sandwich and sips of the
Piels beer, turned to Ryan and Dennis and queried
them on their interests and concerns. Roxy looked up
at one point to find Brendan smirking at her, as if to
say "your boy is doing well." She stuck out her
tongue, which Jonathan noticed, so she had to walk to
the stern and look at the skyline to overcome her
sense of chagrin.

In a moment, Jonathan joined her. "I've got to
hand it to you—it beats Le Cirque," he enthused.

"I'm glad you're having such a terrific time. You're
quite something, you know."

"How so?" he asked.

"Why, you're a natural politician. You've got them
eating out of your hand, and you haven't even kissed
any babies or eaten any corned beef and cabbage yet.
What a future: first you'll build New York and then
you'll rule it."

She turned away from him and he tapped her hard
on the shoulder. "Hey, you," he said. "Stop trying to
bust my chops, OK? You and I have a lot to talk about,
and it's not going to get talked about unless you give
me at least a fighting chance."

She sighed. "Now comes the part where you tell me
how you can have my stripes and have me broken
back to buck private?"

"No. Now comes the time when I tell you that I like your father and your brothers very much—except for your brother Brendan, that is, who makes you look like Shirley Temple—and I have no intention of destroying their world and putting them through the shredder so rich assholes like me can eat crème de menthe ice cream, buy Ralph Lauren underwear, and furnish condos Memphis-style. OK? Do I have to say it again? We can be honest adversaries, but at least let's have some degree of respect for each other."

She was impressed, and also a little afraid, not only for herself, but for the future of her world. "Any tuna sandwiches left?" she asked.

"Yeah," he nodded. "And some hot coffee."

She nodded briskly. "Let's go back to the others," she said. "And we'll see what we can do."

9

STELLA STRODE INTO the lobby of 1185 Park Avenue, her arms filled with yellow roses. She loved her father-in-law's building, a grand residence famous for its gracious atrium entrance, and she could never help thinking how nice it would be to have control of the apartment.

The elevator boy—actually a short Irishman in his sixties—took her up to the eleventh floor. She walked into the apartment and the first thing that hit her was how much it smelled like a hospital. Along with Mrs. Martin, the longtime housekeeper, there was now a strapping black Jamaican nurse in residence, and neither of them seemed particularly happy to see her and her roses.

It was her first visit to the ailing David Broad. She had never had any particular problems with her father-in-law, nor any particular closeness. He wasn't the sort of man who interested her; he had no fire, no dash. Word had it that his wife had been bright and vivacious, famous for her hostessing abilities. It seemed hard to imagine. But she supposed Jonathan had to get his spark from somewhere.

"Is Mr. Broad up to visitors?" she asked Mrs. Martin.

The housekeeper's pinched face narrowed even more. She was a big-bosomed Irishwoman who dressed like Eleanor Roosevelt and who could never help but look askance at Stella's flamboyant wardrobe. "This is generally a time of rest for him," she pronounced.

"I won't be but a minute," Stella promised.

Mrs. Martin led the way down the back hall. The scent of the yellow roses in the confines of the corridor was very strong, but still could not eradicate the fetid odor. This would be short, Stella thought. She hated to be around sickness. It reminded her of her mother, who as a practical nurse had always brought home the smells of her trade. No, the visit, which would be as brief as possible, was simply for Stella to gauge the extent of David's illness with her own two eyes.

Mrs. Martin tiptoed into the dimly lit room. David was lying in bed, looking as white as his sheets. The television was on—"Agronsky and Company," on Channel 13. "Mr. Broad?" Mrs. Martin said. "Your daughter-in-law is here. And look at the lovely roses she's brought."

His bleary eyes turned on them and Stella smiled brilliantly. "Hello, David."

"I'll take those," Mrs. Martin said crisply, and Stella surrendered the roses. When the housekeeper had left, Stella came closer, sitting down in a needlepoint chair by his bedside. She watched him, as he passed in and out of sleep. Poor David, he really looked like death warmed over.

"How are you feeling, dear?" she asked, reaching for his hand. It was cold and clammy and she felt herself recoil, but she told herself that she was an actress and so should act.

Slowly, very slowly, like some kind of ancient lizard, he turned and trained his eye on her. "What do you want?" he whispered.

She was taken aback. Somehow she hadn't expected him to speak. "I just wanted to see how you were doing, David. We've all been so worried about you."

"You've been worried about me," he repeated dully. "That's a laugh."

Now she was shocked. Not only was he lucid when she had expected utter quiescence, but he was nasty, and he'd never been nasty to her. She had read about people undergoing changes in personality during illness, and now she was seeing it with her own eyes.

"Are you uncomfortable, David?" she said. "Can I do something for you?"

"Yes," he said in a voice that was like a croak. "You can get out of my son's life."

She fell back in the chair, as if she'd been slapped across the face.

"Now get out of here," he said, the blood creeping back into his face, "and take your roses with you."

She stood and looked down at him. "The next time I see you," she said, "you'll be quieter."

He pushed the buzzer and the big Jamaican nurse came running. "He seems to be having some sort of seizure," Stella said coolly as she exited.

In the elevator she lit a cigarette, inhaled deeply, and wondered what the ramifications of the whole episode would be. In any case, she had garnered the information she was looking for. She gave him a

126

month, maybe two at the outside. She was heading through the lobby of David Broad's building when she heard someone addressing a question to her.

"What are you doing here?"

It was Jonathan's sister, Merry, dressed in her usual prim little Peck & Peckish going-to-the-office outfit. Minus only the pillbox hat, Stella thought. But her expression was anything but prim.

"I said, What are you doing here?" Merry demanded.

"Visiting your father," said Stella.

"Oh, the angel of mercy. Thanks, but we don't need any."

"And I don't need you to tell me if and when I can visit my father-in-law," Stella challenged.

"Oh, please. Your devotion is sickening," Merry said, walking on.

"You've never given me a chance," Stella said, with a sudden rage for her and all the other "good girls" who wouldn't let her into the club. "Ever since I first met you . . ."

Merry spun around. "You're absolutely right, Stella. I never gave you a chance and I never will. From the moment I laid eyes on you, I knew you were nothing but a cheap tramp who was out to use my brother and the family name to advance herself . . ."

"You bitch," Stella said, wanting to rake her blood-red fingernails across her sister-in-law's smarmy face. "You know what your problem is?"

"I don't want to know," Merry said, turning to go, but Stella gripped her with those nails as strong as talons and held her fixed, like a hen in a hawk's embrace.

"Yes, you do," Stella said. "And I'm going to tell

127

you. You're in love with your brother." Merry pushed at Stella's vise-like grip, but Stella was strong. "You're in love with your brother and you won't let any other man into your pants."

"You sick, pathetic creature," Merry said, in tears. "You're nothing but a cheap whore. I know it and everyone knows it and your time is running out . . ."

Stella smiled and let Merry go. She pulled the lynx coat around her. "I'll see you at the funeral," she said, heading out the door into the crisp autumn air.

The traffic in midtown was a joke, Stella thought, as the car sat on the corner of Fifty-Seventh and Lexington. Lexington Avenue was a joke. The whole city was a joke, a wonderful goddamn joke.

She'd spoken with Gabriel yesterday, and had been told to meet a man wearing blue sunglasses at the Olympic Tower's Delices de Cote Basque installment. She'd told him she would speak soon with Jonathan about the restaurant and saloon interests in River Park, but perhaps after a couple more good fucks, Gabriel would mellow and forget the harebrained scheme. When it came to the mob, the Broads were simply not interested.

At 3:07, Yokimo pulled the jade-green Bentley up to the Olympic Tower. The doorman opened the door for her, and, as she walked into the building, she felt her legs shaking in their thigh-high mauve leather Maxime boots. She wanted those negatives, and every ounce of her adrenalin was churning.

She took a seat in the cafe and looked out at the wall of water that was the centerpiece of the Olympic Tower's public space. It was Jonathan who, even more than Donald Trump, had brought the idea of the usable public space to the city, the idea of building as theatre, and who had restored the sense of vigor that had vanished from the city in the Sixties and Seventies. He was doing one hell of a job, that much she had to give him. Everything would have been so much easier, she thought, if she had loved him.

She pulled out her Bulgari cigarette case. She was smoking so much her teeth were getting yellow. She'd have to go see Dr. Max, who would make her teeth sparkle again. There was nothing you couldn't get fixed in this city if you were willing to pay for it.

Looking around, she saw that at this time of day the only other patrons were two Connecticut ladies with shopping bags from Bergdorf's who looked like they wanted to take their shoes off. She watched them with undisguised interest. What a different species they were from her, she thought. A husband who was a banker or a lawyer or a physician, who came home every night for his dinner of lamb chops and creamed spinach and who maybe went out one night a week for a tennis game or a Masonic Lodge meeting. Two to four children, in school plays and ballet recitals and Little League games. An occasional bridge game with the ladies and committee meetings for the local Children's Hospital and a roll in the hay on Saturday nights after the country club dance. A different sort of life, she thought, with a combination of contempt and something approaching rue.

She glanced at her watch. 3:20. Hailing the waitress, who looked like she went to auditions between shifts, she ordered a coffee, black. She kept looking at the door, waiting for a pair of blue sunglasses to come in.

It had clouded over outside, and she wondered if the man she was waiting for would still be wearing blue sunglasses, and if so what kind of attention he would draw for doing so. When she got the negatives she would burn them on the terrace, and the acrid smoke of burning film would float away and be lost in the polluted air that made for such a pretty sunset.

Would it then be over? Gabriel Messina didn't make such a soft deal. If necessary, she'd tell him of her plans with Wayne Mullins. Then, if he wanted the saloons, he could have the saloons, and the vending machines and the soliciting action too, if he wanted. All she wanted was some time and to know that she was out of this mess, this quicksand.

At 3:27, the revolving door slowly spun around to reveal a tall, thin man, with a long thin face and blue sunglasses. She nodded to him and he made his way over to her, carrying a padded Jiffy mailbag. He sat down at the small white wire table. His legs, when he sat down, were very high, actually above the level of the table. He smiled at her and his teeth were very long and his gums very red. He was an ugly sort of handsome man, she thought, with his too-smooth skin, his lacquered hair, and his lacquered fingernails, and he made the adrenalin pump mightily through her.

"Mrs. Broad?"

"Yes," she said, trying not to stare, but it was almost impossible not to. He was like one of those snakes whose gaze hypnotizes little animals. There was something incredibly sinister about him, a sense of something large and human missing from him altogether.

"Pleasure to meet you," he said. His voice was reedy and much too pleasant for the situation. She felt a peristaltic twisting of her stomach that made her momentarily dizzy.

"You . . . can take off the sunglasses," she whispered. "They might draw attention."

He shrugged. "If you want," he said.

She watched as he slowly, deliberately, removed the blue glasses. He looked at her—one eye was green; the other was opaque, like the white of a poached egg—and he smiled and she held her breath. As she sat there, wondering who this messenger really was and what Gabriel's message really meant, she became aware of the Connecticut ladies wondering what drama was being played out so close by, next to the wall of water, over the two-dollar coffee.

"This is for you," he said, handing her the mailbag.

"Shall I open it?" she said.

"Of course," he replied. "You should always open your presents when they're given to you. Delayed gratification is so unhealthy to the system."

He was clearly not an off-the-streets thug, but some different breed, some kind of mutation with high intelligence and no morals. Morals? Here she was, thinking about morals—an uncustomary posture for her, but one that seemed suddenly unavoidable. She held the mailbag in her hand and, in holding it, felt the palpable, enormously heavy feeling of dread that was contained within its stapled confines. She felt another peristaltic twist of her intestine. Something bad was going to happen.

"What are you waiting for?" he asked.

"What's your name?" she found herself asking,

feeling that if he had a name then he would have a human identity and she wouldn't be so chilled now, even in her lynx coat, so chilled to her very marrow.

"What does it matter?" he asked.

"Just tell me your name," she whispered.

"You can call me Black," he said.

It got her nowhere. It led her down a black corridor through a black tunnel into a bottomless, unfathomable blackness. She felt the place start to tilt and spin, the wall of water seeming ominous, the faces of the Connecticut ladies becoming distorted, as if seen through the wall of water, and the clatter of spoons and dishes, so discreet at first, now hideously rhythmic and disturbing. She held the mailbag in her hands and looked at it and thought she smelled something coming from it, something faintly metallic and sweet and cloying.

"I don't want to," she said.

"Yes, you do," he urged her. "Of course you do."

"I don't want to."

"Do it, Stella."

The invocation of her name was so personal. With trembling fingers, she worked at the staples. Her fingernails weakened them and dug them out and then the mailbag was opened, and she looked at his white eye and his grin and his long teeth, and she pulled out the contents. There were the negatives—at least some of them—but they were damp and red and there were two little packages, plastic wrapped packages, that rolled out onto the white tabletop. She stared at them for a moment, not knowing what they were, and then she looked up at him and he nodded and smiled encouragingly and she looked back at the packages, focusing on them, trying to make sense of them.

132

Inside each packet were dark reddish things. She couldn't figure out what they were except that they looked torn, ragged around the edges, and, almost immediately, obscene to her. She looked up at him again, her lips opened slightly, her chest—her breasts —heaving with the effort of breathing.

He nodded, and she shook her head.

"No," she said.

He smiled. "Think of them as souvenirs," he said, sipping at the glass of water that the waitress had provided him with.

She looked back at the packets. One packet held a finger—a severed finger—and the other packet held a severed ear.

"Souvenirs of Mr. Castriata," he said. "The rest of him will not be found."

"You . . ."

He arched an eyebrow—a mild and quizzical expression that stopped her heart.

"You killed him," she gasped, shading her eyes with her hand.

"Isn't that what you wanted?" he inquired.

"No!" she hissed. "How could you . . . No!"

He sipped again from the water. "There seems to have been a misunderstanding."

"I only wanted the negatives!" she said, wanting to shout down the wall of water, to scream down the tower. "I only wanted you to scare him! You didn't have to kill him."

"But I did have to," the man—Black—said. "And here are half of the negatives and you'll get the other half when you give Gabriel the assurances he's looking for."

She was going to be sick. She was going to be sick

right here, right now. The ear lay at her fingertips, disembodied and grotesque; the finger beckoned like something from the grave. "No," she said brokenly. "That's not what I wanted."

"You can't always get what you want," the man said. He stood and put on the blue sunglasses. "Must run," he said. "Thanks so much." He turned and nodded pleasantly to the Connecticut ladies who were watching the proceedings out of the corners of their eyes.

She felt as if her head would explode. She put the negatives back in the Jiffy bag, and then, holding them by the tips of the plastic wrap packets, the . . . body parts too. Shaking, near to fainting, she rose and rushed past the Connecticut ladies into the ladies' room where, on her knees in the stall, she vomited. For a long moment, she lay there with her forehead against the cool white porcelain.

_____**10**

JONATHAN WAS ON the phone thanking Mike Mulligan, the *News* columnist, for his latest piece when Lotte came in looking very unhappy.

"Hang up," she said.

"Mike, I'll catch you later," Jonathan said, and hung up the phone. "What's up?"

"What's down," she replied, deadpan. "In the street, floating across the moat, darling, and into the courtyard—don't ask."

"Come on, Lotte, give," he said.

"A demonstration. Led by one Mr. Sherman Maloney."

"Oh, Jesus."

"No, I don't think Jesus is involved as of yet, but it looks like just about everybody else is. I was coming back from lunch when I saw the busloads disembark and, Lord, you've never seen a ratpack like this before. It looks like the Reverend Jim Jones's bunch has been reincarnated and landed on our doorstep. This is the ragged army, Jonathan—handicapped, oldsters, Rastafarians. Believe me, with Ivan Malagorsky on the Steinway grand in the background, it's really something."

Jonathan jumped up and began to pace around the room. "Real funny, Lotte. Like a broken crutch."

"Don't mention the word 'crutch,'" she said. "That's all you'll see when you go downstairs."

Damn it, he thought, as the elevator made its descent. He really needed this, on top of all the machinations he was going through with River Park, on top of his father's illness, on top of his problems with Stella.

"Quite a scene out there, Mr. Broad," said Phil, the elevator operator.

"So I hear," said Jonathan.

"I don't know what them people want," Phil continued. "Like they can't expect time to stand still or nothin', right?"

"Well, we'll see what they have to say," Jonathan said with as much equanimity as he could muster.

As the elevator doors opened on the promenade level, he was confronted with a scene out of Breughel. There must have been three hundred pickets, most of whom looked like they'd been found sleeping in doorways, and they were carrying crude, hand-painted signs. ROBBER BARON RAPES CITY. OUT WITH THE POOR—IN WITH THE YUPPIES. BROAD MUST BE STOPPED.

Catching sight of him, the crowd broke into a cacophony of catcalls and insults. "Is Sherman Maloney here?" Jonathan called. A small balding man, wearing a dumpy brown suit and blue Nikes, came forward.

"I think it's time we talked, Mr. Maloney," Jonathan said, indicating the elevator and the upper sanctum where they would confer.

Maloney turned to the crowd and raised a clenched

fist. "I shall return," he announced. Flashbulbs went off; TV cameras clustered around as he joined Jonathan in the elevator.

"That's quite a crowd you've got out there, Mr. Maloney," Jonathan remarked.

"Yeah," said Maloney. "The naked and the dead. The sorts of folks you never get to meet, huh, Broad?"

"Not too often," he admitted.

"I think it's a crying shame," said Phil, with the outrage of a house retainer seeing his master impugned, "for you people to come in here and make a mess."

"Ah, who asked you?" said Maloney, his round, lumpy face aglow with contentiousness.

"That's okay, Phil," said Jonathan gently. "Mr. Maloney and I have a lot to talk about."

The elevator opened, revealing the expanse of glass wall that gave way to one of the most staggering skyviews in the world. Jonathan watched Sherman Maloney's eyes widen. He had probably never seen a view like this before, except from the observation deck of the Empire State Building.

"Please, Mr. Maloney," Jonathan said. "Come this way." Jonathan led him down the carpeted hallway, hung with Abstract Expressionist paintings by the likes of Clyfford Still, Barnett Newman, and Mark Rothko. As they headed past Lotte, Jonathan stopped. "Lotte Gurwitz," he said, "Mr. Sherman Maloney."

Lotte extended her hand. "A pleasure," she said. "Can I get you something?"

"Yeah," said Maloney. "Coffee. Extra light. Four sugars."

She glanced at Jonathan, who fought to suppress a smile. "Coming right up," she growled.

It was midafternoon and the western light was streaming into his office at just the right angle, turning the wood-paneled walls honey gold. "Nice place you got here, Broad," said Maloney, settling into a Breuer chair—at least as much as one *can* settle into a Breuer chair.

"Glad you like it," Jonathan said. "Cigar?" he asked, offering a Montecruz from the ebony humidor.

Maloney reached in and withdrew two, pocketing one and lighting up the other. In another moment Lotte entered with the coffee in a Spode eggshell china cup, and then they were ready to begin.

"So, Mr. Maloney," said Jonathan, leaning back in his chair. "It seems I'm doing something you'd rather I didn't do."

"That's a nice way to put it, Broad," said Maloney, through a veil of smoke. "But I'd put it a different way. I'd say you're doing something that is downright criminal."

"How so?"

"You're putting people out of their homes. That kind of thing went out with the silent screen villains. You know, the ones who tied girls to the railroad tracks."

"Look at me, Mr. Maloney," Jonathan said. "You see any black handlebar moustache for me to twirl? You see any evil leer?"

"The fact you're clean-cut doesn't make a whit of difference," Maloney said. "You're still looking to pull the carpet out from under us."

"Who's 'us'?" Jonathan demanded to know.

Maloney stared at his growing, marvelously suspended cigar ash for a long moment before answering.

138

"First it was just the folks in my building. None of us had anywhere to go. Some of your flunkeys came around offering twenty grand a head if we'd clear out and go to Long Beach like nice little boys and girls. But I twisted everybody's arm not to. And it wasn't easy, let me tell you. Boy, we got some stupid folks in our building. They saw twenty thousand green ones and they figured this was Oz and they were over the rainbow. Yeah, over the rainbow with a one-way ticket—coach class. It just wasn't good enough. So I told 'em hang on. Where someone is willing to give twenty, then they'll give more . . ."

"Now just a minute, Mr. Maloney," said Jonathan. This was one garrulous old coot, with grand visions that were going to be a headache to keep under control.

"No, *you* just wait a minute, Mr. Broad," Maloney said, filling the room with cigar smoke. "You think just 'cause you've got a fancy view and Cuban cigars you're gonna turn my head or something but don't count on it. I was a court reporter for forty years, did you know that?"

"So I heard."

"So you heard, huh? I've seen them all. Dutch Schultz, Carmine De Sapio, Joseph Bonanos, they were all in my courtroom. So don't expect me to go all gaga over a few amenities, OK? If there's one thing in life I know, buster, it's that the mighty will fall."

"Are you here to insult me to my face, Mr. Maloney," Jonathan said firmly, "or do you want to talk turkey?"

"Well, now. That's a refreshing approach for somebody like you," the old man said, stirring in his chair.

"Now I'll tell you the rest. You sent your boys around with the twenty grand and all the feebs in my building started doing the hula over it, they were so damned excited. I told them twenty grand wouldn't buy them a linen closet in Miami Beach and they say, 'But it's more money than we ever seen in our whole lives.' I tell them, 'Listen, turkeys, you never seen more than fifty bucks and some green stamps at any one time in your life, but you got to hold out. You are controlled tenants—he cannot put you out on the street. You've got the power, turkeys,' I told them."

"And they listened to you?" Jonathan said, with no little amazement.

"Sure they listened to me," Maloney said proudly. "Why shouldn't they listen to me? You know who I'm talking about here? Hod carriers. Merchant seamen. Seamstresses. Retired hooch dancers. If it wasn't for my dear wife's illness wiping out my life savings, I wouldn't be anywhere near this bunch, but here I am and I'm like God to them because I know the letter of the law. And after I got through making the tenants in my building sign a no-sell pledge, I went to other buildings I heard about where your boys were selling their snake oil . . ."

"Now, Mr. Maloney," said Jonathan patiently, "I know this all seems like a lot of fun to you . . ."

"Fun?" Maloney cried. "Who the hell thinks it's fun? I'm out there saving my neck and the necks of people like me. Do you care about us, Mr. Broad?" he challenged.

"Of course I do. Don't you think . . ."

"No—really. Do you really care about us?" Maloney said, throwing the question at him again.

Jonathan stared into Maloney's rheumy old eyes. "What do you want, Mr. Maloney? River Park's not going to go away—not with three hundred pickets, not with three thousand. So why don't you tell me what you want?"

Maloney took a few puffs off the cigar before answering. "I don't want twenty grand, I don't want thirty, I don't want forty . . ."

"You couldn't possibly want more than that," Jonathan said. "It's unthinkable for you to expect more than that."

"I don't want your money, Broad," Maloney spat.

"Then what is it you want?"

"I want your assurances that we will have a place to live," Maloney said forthrightly. "A decent place, with heat and running water, free of rats of the human and the animal variety."

Jonathan considered this silently for a moment. "How do you propose this happen, Mr. Maloney?" he asked.

"Make a percentage of every luxury building you put up in the complex part-subsidized for low-income tenants. Put in ramps for the handicapped. Show us that you're serious about people and not just about making money."

"You're a tough character, Mr. Maloney," Jonathan said, as he rose. "If you call off your troops, I'd appreciate it. And I want to keep a dialogue going with you."

"Dialogue?" said Sherman Maloney, his wizened face screwing up into a grimace. "Keep that for the actors and actresses. As far as I'm concerned, the ball's in your court, Broad."

* * *

At seven he went upstairs to change for the evening. Stella was already in the master bedroom suite, itself as large as your average one-bedroom apartment. She stood in front of her dressing room mirror, holding a silk gown of scarlet paisley—an Emanuel Ungaro, bought for nine thousand—against her naked body, and some kind of red feather headdress against her head.

"What are you going as?" Jonathan asked. "Sitting Bull?"

"Up yours," she said. "If you don't like it, stay home."

They were going to the big Diana Ross opening at the Silver Lode Casino in Atlantic City. It was a benefit performance, with the proceeds going to the Joseph & Mary Children's Hospital of Camden. Stella was out to look her best and, for her, her best translated to no underwear.

"Put something on underneath that dress," he said.

"Don't you dare tell me what to do," she said, stepping into the gown.

"I said put something on."

"The underwear ruins the line of the dress," she explained.

"It may ruin the line of the dress," he said, "but it keeps you from looking like the sort of $100-a-night hooker we try to keep out of our hotels."

She threw the dress aside and stood there, her hands on her hips, a lascivious smile on her lips. "What's the matter, Johnny?" she said. "Don't want the other men to see my apples?"

He stared at her and felt something stir in his groin. He shook his head, wanting to shake her away. "I forget sometimes where I found you."

"You knew what I was," she said, "someone who could show you a good time . . . and did. It was only when you tried to make me into something I'm not that we ran into trouble."

"What are you?" he said, in a low, throbbing voice. "Just what the hell are you?"

She looked at him and then she smiled. Teasingly, provocatively, she lifted her breasts and played with them, smiling all the while like a stripper with a hot act. Her nipples stuck out like valves, and he wanted to take them between his fingers and squeeze them till they hurt. While he was watching her—he couldn't look away—she turned her back to him, leaned over, and looking behind her, began to play with her sex and rotate her hips and buttocks, smiling all the while, even laughing.

He couldn't stay away, as much as he wanted to, as much as he wanted to avoid forever that hold she had on him. "Stop it," he said, his voice low, urgent.

"I can't," she said, with a bewitching moan. "And why should I?"

He went to where she was, and she met him by pressing her naked buttocks against him. "Do it, Johnny," she breathed. "For old time's sake."

He hesitated, and she turned, and rose, and pressed her hot lips against him, her hungry tongue that searched in his mouth for his sweet secret. Then he felt her firm, probing hands on him, and then he went at her, with a mix of desire and lust and fury. He pulled her to the floor and they devoured each other, making wild animal noises, and when he was driving into her she laughed with the most uninhibited ripple of delight and even mockery. He plunged deeper into her, as deep as his desire would take him. "There," he

143

said, as he bucked against her. "Take it! There!" She groaned and met him with shivers and tremors that converted her whole body with a kind of fit, a paroxysm of sheer abandoned orgasm.

"Oh, that was good," she said, more pleasantly than she had said anything to him in months. "We ought to do that more often."

He looked away, feeling sickened by his own admission of weakness.

"But you got me all mussed," she said coyly. "I'm going to have to take another bath now and we'll be late."

"Forget about it," he said hollowly.

"Forget about it?" she cried. "I can't go to the big party with the smell of your come all over me, can I? What will people say? They'll think we're in love or something." With that, she let go a peal of laughter, and he left her there.

Stella clutched Jonathan's arm. There were few things in the world of which she was afraid— helicopters, dangling over New York City, happened to be one of them. "Get it together," he said irritably, not wanting to be touched by her. "Just look at the view."

"Screw the view," she said. "If I look down there, I'm going to lose it, right here, right now, on your shoe."

He stared at her. How could a woman as beautiful as she was be so utterly coarse. He had known very little about her when they got married. She told him her parents had died when she was very young, and that she had been raised by a family friend. To get around her past, she told him that she was terrified of big weddings, and so they'd made it an intimate affair in his father's apartment, with just the immediate family in attendance. She had looked incomparably beautiful in a white wool Chanel suit, and her aspect could not have been sweeter. It stayed sweet for a fairly long time, when she was the little woman at his side, and then later, when she became his right hand and he gave her the hotels to run. Once that was under her belt, the other, darker, side of her personality emerged from under its tight wraps. There began to be fierce nightly arguments about money and autonomy. Making a family became a new battlefield; she wasn't "ready." When would she be ready? She'd let him know.

He looked at her now, and felt loathing bubble up in his throat like bile. She wasn't what Lotte would call a *mensch*—a human being. She was base and low and cared nothing about anyone but herself.

"Why are you looking at me so funny?" she demanded, pulling her sable coat around her.

He shook his head. "I don't know."

"Thinking naughty thoughts?" she grinned.

"No."

"Oh, come on. Admit it—you loved it. You're getting so damned glum. Just like your father . . ."

"Shut up," he said.

"Oooh," she cried, in mock fear. "Don't get angry just because the holy name of David Broad has been caressed by my filthy lips."

"I said, shut up!"

She laughed. "Oh, Jonathan, sometimes you're such a big baby. The world thinks you're so mighty, the master builder. But only a wife knows the real secrets . . ."

"You're not my wife," he said. "You're married to me but you're not my wife."

"Watch it," she said, her grin evaporating. "You don't want to say anything you'll be sorry for." She looked down below. "There's the Palisades," she said, changing the subject and pointing to the Broad Hotel under construction on the waterfront. This would ultimately fit into the River Park scheme but had been undertaken as a separate entity. "Isn't it lovely this time of night?" she said, momentarily forgetting her queasiness.

"Yeah," he said grimly, "it's terrific."

The copter lit down in New Jersey and a car met them to whisk them away to the Casino. Inside the Rolls Jonathan watched a Giants-Oilers game on tape as Stella glared at him. "Do you have to have that crap on?" she said finally.

He ignored her.

She reached over and turned it off.

"What do you think you're doing?"

"I want to talk to you."

"I don't," he said, putting it back on.

She took out a cigarette and lit it.

"I've told you I don't want smoking in this car," he said.

She puffed away.

He couldn't stand it anymore. He turned off the TV; she put out her cigarette. "OK," he said. "What do you want to talk about?"

She smiled, and reached out to touch his thigh. "Jonathan, I've been thinking about River Park . . ."

"It has nothing to do with you," he said.

She digested that for a moment, buried it, continued in her staunch fashion. "There are more strings to pull than you've been pulling," she said. "If you want to put this thing across, there are avenues you haven't explored."

"Are you telling me how to run my business?" he said.

"Don't be a fool. You may not think you have much use for me, but one thing you ought to know about me by now is that I'm worth listening to."

She was right, Jonathan thought. She had a shrewd mind, and, in the past, had come up with some tactics, often ruthless, that would not have occurred to him. "OK," he said. "Talk."

"Monday I had lunch with Demetria Koulivourdas," she said, naming the daughter of a fabulously rich Greek shipping magnate, "and she invited along a friend of hers, a restaurateur named Gabriel Messina. He's been hugely successful out on the coast, owns his own vineyards, poultry farms, produce farms. Wants to break into New York, and promised me that if we could throw him the River Park restaurant business, he would produce something so fantastic that we would never want to sign a contract with anyone else."

She looked up at him. The performance was a difficult one; there's only so much you can do with a poor script, she thought.

He gave her a long hard look. "What are you talking about?" he said.

"Well, Demetria vouched for him all the way down the line. Said he was a genius, that he . . ."

"What are you talking about?" he repeated. "Gabriel Messina is the head of a Mafia family. Do you think I could be as significant a part of this city as I am and not know something like that?"

Uncharacteristically, she was at a loss. What could she say? *Oh, he is?* "I think he's gone legitimate, Jonathan," she said. "Demetria told me that . . ."

"Cut the shit!" he snapped. "What kind of a jerk do you take me for? Demetria told you . . . Bullshit! You could run circles around Demetria Koulivourdas. Now what were you doing with Gabriel Messina?"

She looked away for a moment. But she hadn't gotten where she was by not knowing how to collect herself. She was a survivor. "All right," she said, looking back at him, "I approached Messina myself."

"What!" This time he was truly shocked.

"That's right. I got tired of watching you pussyfoot from one two-bit bureaucrat to the next . . ."

He laughed. "I don't seem to have had any problem in the past without your help."

"This is bigger than anything else you've ever tried," she said. "I don't think you even know how big. You want to get this thing going, then do it right."

"The Broad Company does not go to bed with the mob," Jonathan said, his hand slicing through the air for emphasis. "Not now, not ever."

"There is no deal to be made on the waterfront without cultivating the right kind of friends," she spat. "When are you going to grow up? When are you going to stop being the best little boy for your daddy and the white knight for your simp sister and Mr. Wonderful for the whole goddamn world?"

Like a flash, his hand reached out and slapped her across the face as hard as it could. He had never struck a woman before, but he felt good doing it and didn't even consider making an apology for it.

"Does that make you happy?" she asked, touching

148

her cheek, tears in her eyes despite her every effort to keep them away.

"Yeah," he said. "Real good. Thanks for asking."

"Don't judge me, Jonathan Broad. A man who hits a woman—you're in no position to judge me."

"You'd better put some make-up on that, Stella," he said coldly. "You don't want to make an appearance looking like someone gave you what you deserve."

"You're a bastard," she screamed, not caring if the chauffeur heard, "a lousy little bastard. Always had it easy, everybody doting on you, kissing your stinking little feet! Well, I hope your whole world falls apart. I hope you wind up like your father—a vegetable!"

He wanted to smash her face again, but this time he controlled himself. "Pull yourself together, Stella. Tonight is our last appearance together. After tonight, you're through. I don't care what kind of shame or money it's going to cost me."

"It'll cost you plenty," she said. "I'll tell all your little secrets. I'll tell how you beat me . . ."

"Oh, you're an actress, kid, but not a very good one . . ."

"Good enough to fool you, sap," she said, rubbing her cheek.

"Right. But not good enough to make it to the top. This is where you get off the ladder, and in a few months no one will remember your name. I'll see to it."

"I *am* at the top," she swore, "and I intend to stay there. And if I don't," she said, reaching in her bag for her compact, "I'll drag you down with me. As God is my witness, I'll drag you down with me."

11

IT WAS MIDDAY in the office when Jonathan heard that his father had taken a turn for the worse and had been rushed back to Mount Sinai. Jonathan had been in a meeting with Anderson Kendall, and Anderson insisted on accompanying him to the hospital. "It really isn't necessary, Anderson," said Jonathan, shaken.

"Let him go," said Lotte, overhearing the exchange. "It's no good sitting in a hospital corridor by yourself. I know. I've been there."

Jonathan looked at Anderson, whose entire demeanor indicated a willingness to serve. "OK, Andy," he said, "let's go."

"I'll tell Sidney you guys went off together," Lotte called after them with a mischievous grin.

The traffic uptown was snarled, as usual. "Shall we go over the numbers on the Morningside Heights deal?" Jonathan said, referring to a big co-op conversion that Anderson was handling up near Columbia University.

"If you want," Anderson said, and he began to spout figures. But Jonathan shook his head. "No, I can't deal with it now. Sorry."

Anderson nodded sympathetically. "No reason why you should, Jonathan."

"He's a fighter," Jonathan said. "But I know in my heart that he's not going to win this fight."

"I don't know," said Anderson. "David is an extraordinary man. He's probably the most unflappable person I've ever met. He never compromises his values, never jumps on any bandwagon . . ."

"That's my father," Jonathan agreed. "Some people have called him phlegmatic, even stolid, and maybe he is. But he's also bedrock." He turned to look at Anderson, whose handsome face was a study in concern. "I don't know what I'm going to do without him, Andy."

"We're all here to support you, Jonathan," he said.

Jonathan was grateful. He prided himself on his fairness in his dealings with his associates, and they were a fine group. But he had never grown personally close to any of them. Perhaps one reason for that was that his father's insistence had always drummed into him and his sister that there was the family and then there were others. The others, as good and worthwhile as they might be, must never be made party to any real intimacies. But now, sitting here with Anderson, who had joined the firm three years ago and who had proved himself to be gifted and likable and loyal, Jonathan was reconsidering his father's dictum. "The thing that was always so special to me about my father was the feeling of complete acceptance I got from him. I could do no wrong. I was the best and the brightest . . ."

"But in fact you were, Jonathan." Anderson grinned.

Jonathan shook his head. "No, I wasn't. There were always plenty of people better than I was. Why, you went to the Business School"—meaning Harvard, of course—"and you did better than I did. But it didn't matter, because I never worried about failing. And now, looking at the possibility of his being gone, I do feel, for the first time in my life, that failure is a real possibility."

"Would it be so terrible if you did fail at something?" Andérson asked gently.

"Yes. It would. I don't know how to do it." He looked at his watch. "Damned traffic. Can't you go any faster, Fergus?"

"Only if I drive on the sidewalk, sir," the chauffeur returned.

"I worry too about Merry," Jonathan confessed. "She's in Acapulco now—first vacation she's taken in years. I'm not going to call her back until I have to."

"No," Anderson agreed. "She needs the rest. She's been working like a demon."

Jonathan looked at Anderson. You thought Anderson was an aristocrat, terribly above it all, and then you got to know him as a person and appreciated his wry sense of humor and his natural class. He wished that Anderson would show an interest in Merry and had tried to promote this in a low-keyed way, inviting them together on the yacht some afternoons and so forth, but it had never clicked.

"Tell me, Andy," he said, "as a favor. It'll go no further. Is there some reason why Merry's not attractive to men?"

Anderson was clearly taken aback and seemed to be weighing his options before answering. But finally, he chose one of those options—honesty—and gave Jonathan an answer. "She doesn't seem interested in men, Jonathan. Men out of the family, that is. Whenever I speak to her she seems focused only on what the Broad men are up to."

Jonathan nodded heavily. "Thank you for your honesty, Andy," he said. In a way, the question had been a test for Anderson and he'd passed the test, despite the unfortunate light his honesty shed on Merry.

David's physician, Dr. Korsmeyer, was waiting outside David's room in the intensive care unit. "I'm sorry," Dr. Korsmeyer told Jonathan. "He's failing."

"But . . . what can we do?" Jonathan cried.

"We're doing everything we can."

The first thing Jonathan did was place a call to Merry, but she was away from her hotel. Returning to his father's room, he went to stand beside his father's bed.

"Pop?" he asked. "Can you hear me?"

David Broad's breathing was labored; there was a fluttering behind his eyelids. Already, he seemed so far away.

"Listen to me, Pop," he cried. "You can pull through this. I know you can."

But it was empty talk. The coma had descended and, barring some miracle, there would be no reversal. He took his father's old, spotted hand in his own; the coldness of it momentarily repelled him and then he lowered his head so that it was pressed against it. With a sudden paroxysm of emotion, he broke and the shuddering sobs came. He was like that for a long time, so lost in his emotions that at first he hardly noticed when Anderson came behind him and threw an arm around his shoulders.

"I only hope he doesn't stay on this way for long," Jonathan said. "He wouldn't have wanted this. To be helpless like this . . ."

Anderson gave him a reassuring squeeze on the shoulder. "Things have a way of working out for the best."

Jonathan, grateful for the wise words of his friend, managed a nod. "Thank you for being here, Anderson," he said. "It helps."

"That's what I'm here for, Jonathan."

Stella sat up in bed smoking her cigarette. Don't smoke in bed, the song went, but she'd always broken the rules and always would.

She got up and went to the bathroom. It was a nice place he had, she thought. Conservative, masculine—she felt comfortable here. She hadn't been here too many times, half a dozen maybe, over the course of six months. This was not a wildly passionate affair. It was a useful affair—useful for both of them. And the nice thing was that he made a very good lover. He was considerate and virile and he kept himself in fine shape. All that squash at the Harvard Club paid off.

She went back into the bedroom and gazed at his sleeping form. Of all her lovers at the moment—and there were three—he was, by a country mile, the most beautiful.

"Wake up, sweetie," she murmured, kissing his ear, as perfectly formed and pink as a conch shell.

He squirmed, tried to wriggle away from her.

She kissed down from his ear, along his neck, to his nipple. "Oh, Stella," he groaned.

154

Watching his cock grow, she felt pleased. "Come on, Anderson, wake up."

He yawned and sat up in bed. "Mmnh, that was just what the doctor ordered after a long day at the office."

"And the hospital," she added naughtily.

"You're too much, Stella," he murmured. "Better than a chiropractor."

"You think so?" she asked with a crooked little grin.

He nodded. "Most everyone at Broad thinks of you as a bitch on wheels, but I for one know that there is more to Madame than that."

"How nicely put," she cooed. "And screw everyone at Broad. Pretty soon it'll be in our hands anyway."

"You really think so?" he asked, as she massaged the tight muscles in his neck.

"I really think so," she assured him. "Without Daddy in the background, Jonathan'll fall apart. You don't understand that family. It's not a family—it's a clan. You take out one of the stones and the whole thing'll fall apart. And you, me, and assorted friends will be there to pick up the pieces." She leaned down to kiss him.

"Stella, you're amazing," he said. "But sometimes I think you don't want me for myself. Sometimes I think you're just using me as a tool."

"You're an excellent tool," she said drily. "Don't knock it."

"That's not what I mean . . ."

"I know what you mean, baby," she said. "But, to tell you the truth, you and I are very much alike. We both know what we want and we're both going after it. Why do I want you, beside the fact that you're a handsome young stud who can service me?" He laughed and took her into his arms. "Because Jona-

155

than thinks you're his loyal friend. And because, knowing you as I now do, I've come to understand that the only friend Anderson Kendall has is Anderson Kendall . . ."

"Hey now."

"Don't worry about it, baby. I've no problem with it. You and I will form a very nice partnership and together we'll see to it that there are no Broads in the Broad Company. You tell me all your secrets, and I'll tell you all mine."

He stared at her. "Let's shake on it."

"No," she said, lying back langorously. "Let's do something else on it."

As she left Anderson's and headed toward the plum-colored Lamborghini parked over on Third Avenue, someone came up behind her. As she turned, the man grabbed her, covering her mouth, and pushed her toward a waiting car. She fought furiously, trying to bite his hand, but he put pressure on her carotid artery and she blacked out for a moment. When she regained consciousness, she was within the dark and plush interior of a limousine and Gabriel Messina was staring at her.

"My God," she said, wanting to try out her voice, fearing that something had been broken. "What are you doing? Are you crazy?"

"The question is what are *you* doing?" He was drinking something—Strega, she thought—and something operatic was on in the background.

"How could you put a thug on me like that," she demanded, "after what we've been through together . . ."

156

"You're not playing, darling. This is not a game, this is life. I wanted you to know how it feels."

"What do you want from me?" she burst out.

"You know what I want," he said coldly.

"I came to you for help. I offered myself to you. And then you extracted a promise from me that I've tried to keep but I don't know if I can keep it!" she cried. The shock of the intrusion—the abduction— was hitting her now and she felt wild and desperate.

"You've got to keep your promises," he said. "That's the most important thing in the whole world. Didn't your mother teach you that?"

"Gabriel, please . . ."

"You were going to get me the restaurants," he said blandly. "You were going to get me the bars."

"I spoke to Jonathan about it," she said. "He wouldn't budge. You have to understand Jonathan's father and his grandfather. Old Jan Broot—he was a Dutch plasterer. A good Dutch burgher. How can you think . . ."

"I don't want history," Gabriel said, sipping his liqueur, "I want action."

"I'm trying to explain something to you," she babbled. "Let me explain."

"No," he said, leaning close to her. "I'll explain to you. I am Gabriel Messina. I am one of the most powerful men in this country. You are Stella Nevins Broad. You are a two-bit chippie who's gotten in over her head . . ."

She stared at him. Her heart was pounding. This couldn't be. This was a nightmare. She tried to think of who she could turn to, who was more powerful than Gabriel, but there was no one. He could make her his

157

slave if he wanted to. She felt terribly cold all of a sudden and began to shiver.

"I'll take care of this matter myself," he said. "I'll go to your husband and I will broach a business arrangement that I am sure he'll find attractive."

She felt momentarily relieved. "Do that, Gabriel," she said. "My hands are tied. I've done all I can."

She tried in vain to read his expression. "That man . . . the other day," she said. "He only brought half the negatives."

Gabriel smiled, showing his dazzling white teeth. "He said you seemed nervous. He said you didn't like the sight of blood."

Her heart raced on. "I didn't . . . you didn't tell me you were going to . . . eliminate him."

"Eliminate," Gabriel repeated, chewing on the word. "You've been reading too many James Bond novels. We use the word 'kill.'"

She forced herself to look up at him. "You didn't tell me you were going to kill him."

"You didn't ask. You told me you wanted the situation resolved. I resolved the situation."

"Where are the rest of the negatives?"

He reached into an attaché case and pulled out an envelope.

She reached for them, and, like a whip, he sliced the envelope through the air and smashed it against her face. She yelped and cringed away from him. "Not so fast," he said softly.

"You said you'd give them to me," she said, hearing herself whine.

"On conditions," he reminded her. She watched as he pulled the negatives from the envelope. "Anyway," he said, "I like to look at them." He held up the negatives to the light. "Look at that," he sniggered. "Man, you've got a talent."

At the worst moments of her life—when her stepfather was using her night after night—she hadn't felt as degraded as she did now. She tried not to—but she couldn't help it—she burst into tears.

"What are you crying about?" he said.

She just kept crying, great wracking sobs pouring out of her.

"Oh, Christ. I can't stand to see a woman cry," he said, his voice unmistakably wry.

She looked up at him. "What do you want?" she said. "What can I do?"

"Do what you do best," he advised.

She didn't know what he meant. She looked at him blankly, awaiting his direction.

"Take your clothes off," he said.

She lost her breath. Her heart seemed to leap within her like a trapped animal. "What do you mean?"

"What do you mean what do I mean?" he shouted. His face, usually so smooth, so urbane, had turned suddenly monstrous. In their time together in the past, he had never shown any of this. Was he going mad? What could she do?

"Please, Gabriel . . ."

He reached out, grabbed a hank of her long black hair, and wound it around his meaty hand. "Take off your clothes," he hissed.

She was terrified. Tentatively, she began to undo the buttons of her silk blouse, but not fast enough to please her captor, who reached out and ripped it. It was as if he were ripping her flesh. As she winced in fear he ground his lips against hers. "Don't," she murmured.

159

He tore at her silk pants, getting them down around her knees, and then he ripped away her sinfully expensive lace panties. "Don't you tell me 'don't'," he grunted in her ear. "You do what I say when I say it and you smile when you do it." It was like having a beast upon her.

"You're hurting me . . ."

"I'll hurt you more."

He rose and undid his belt. He lowered his pants and then his undershorts, exposing an erection more massive than she had ever seen from him before. It was not like her to be afraid of anything that had to do with sex, but it was clear to her that he had pain in mind.

"Suck it, bitch."

She hesitated for a moment and again he wound her hair around his hand and pulled her head forward, forcing himself between her lips and then out again and then in. "You can do better than that," he said.

She did better. She did as well as she could. She was fighting for her life, because he wanted to destroy her.

"Fine lady," he muttered contemptuously. "Fancy clothes. Fancy furs. I knew you when, Stella Nevins."

Brutally, he threw her back on the seat and raised up her legs. With a sneer of vindictiveness on his face, he entered her. She was dry, dry with fear, and he was furious. "The first goddamn time in your life you've been that way," he shouted.

She moved for him, doing anything to make it easier. As he plunged in and out, she felt seared. He pulled and plucked at her nipples, bit ruthlessly at her neck, pinched her buttocks to make her scream.

160

"That's right, baby. Scream! Scream!" he shouted, as he neared his climax, and then, with a roar, he came, and collapsed on her, lying there for a long moment. Then he roused himself and pulled himself off her. "You're Gabriel Messina's property now," he told her.

She wanted to scream again in protest, in fury. But she kept her mouth shut. She watched as he picked up the cell phone and placed a call. "Gabriel Messina for Jonathan Broad," he said.

She watched in horror. "What are you doing?" she cried.

He ignored her thoroughly; she didn't exist for him unless he wanted her to exist. "You tell him that Gabriel Messina wants to meet him tomorrow at eight A.M. at the tower in Jones Beach. Have you got that? Good."

He hung up, and looked over at her. Picking up her ripped clothes, he balled them in his fist. "Put your coat on," he ordered.

She couldn't seem to move.

"Put your coat on!"

She pulled on her lynx coat.

He handed her the ripped garments. "Now get out," he said.

"Why are you doing this to me?" she said, trembling.

"Because I want you to know who I am and who you are," he said. "Now get out, and when I need you I'll get you."

She got out onto the street, naked beneath her coat, and watched the car pull away. She was on Twelfth Avenue, near the river. It was late and there were people, dangerous people, looking at her. She walked quickly, trying not to run, because if she ran they would smell her fear and they would be upon her. She headed up the street, her high-heeled shoes making a tattoo on the sidewalk, as she gave into the impulse and raced into the night.

12

THERE IS NOTHING lonelier than a hospital at six o'clock in the morning. Particularly, Jonathan thought, when you were waiting for someone to die. The only change in his father, as he lay deep in the coma, was a gradual withering, as though the life-blood was draining out of him. In the comfortable seat nearest to the bed was the sleeping figure of Merry. She had gotten back a few days ago. On her return from vacation she had told him furiously that he'd had no right to keep this from her, but then the argument had ended as quickly as it had begun as they collapsed into each other's arms.

Now Merry passed days in that chair, keeping a vigil by her father's bedside that she would not allow anyone to disturb. She would not leave the hospital until it was over. And who knew; it could be days, or months.

He looked at her and thought about what Anderson had said: the only men in the world who existed for her were the men in her family. He thought about how he had always gotten the attention, prepped to be the golden boy, and how Merry had always been right there in the cheering squad. Now he realized that the responsibility for his sister would be on him. Would she ever marry? Would she ever have children? Would *he* ever have children? Would all the energy and purpose of the Broads die out with this generation?

He had spoken to his lawyer and announced his plans to get rid of Stella as soon, and as cleanly, as possible. For now, they were on opposite wings of their endless apartment, and he hadn't even seen her for the last three days. He felt better than he had in ages.

The very thought of what she was into was enough to curdle his blood. At first he was inclined to disregard the message from Gabriel Messina, but whatever slime Stella was into could not be kept bottled up; he might as well confront that truth now.

Taking a last look at Merry and his father, he went downstairs and got into the car that would take him out to Jones Beach. It was a dark blue Audi, a conservative, inconspicuous car that he kept on hand for those sorts of occasions. "Let's go, Fergus," he said, turning his attention to the *Forbes, Barron's,* and *Fortune* magazines that he collected for his limousine time.

But today he found himself unable to concentrate on what was at hand, his mind reeling. He told himself a period of crisis was good. After all, he had ambitions toward politics, and part of that task would involve being able to cope with crises in a sober and constructive way. When he thought of men like Truman and Kennedy and Reagan, he thought first of the way they were able to handle crises with grace under pressure.

"I think I'll take Meadowbrook Parkway, sir," said Fergus in his thick Irish brogue. "Less traffic."

"Whatever you say, Fergus," Jonathan replied.

Fergus was very special, very valuable. Not only did he know which routes had less traffic on them, not only could he keep his mouth shut about his sentry duty outside Abigail Forester's home, but he had another, even more significant value. He was a fully trained antiterrorist bodyguard. A veteran of the Irish Republican Army, he had a sixth sense for sudden violence. Jonathan always had the feeling about him, fair or not, that Fergus could smell a bomb a mile away. He carried a Berettz Modello 9mm, was a crack marksman, and a black belt in karate. Although violence had not entered into Jonathan's life, he had had to admit that the potential for violence surrounding a man of his wealth was manifold, which is why he hired protection. Now, en route to a meeting in a remote place with a Mafia chieftain, he felt protected.

He wondered what Messina would have to say. He knew already, from Stella, that Messina wanted into the restaurant and bar business, but what was going to be his bargaining chip? What did Messina think he had on Jonathan? Messina must have thought he had something good—good enough for him to schedule a meeting in this place, so early in the morning, and to feel sure that Jonathan would come.

They paid their toll at Jones Beach and pulled out onto the causeway. The last time he had come, maybe the only time, was to see his friend Joe Namath starring in *Damn Yankees;* Jonathan had gotten together a bunch of fans for the outing. Here, at 7:45 on an overcast October morning, Jones Beach had a very different, almost sinister, look.

They drove down the broad thoroughfares, the smell of the ocean wafting into the car, the beach grasses swaying in the wind. This was the dream project of one man: Robert Moses, the Czar of New York, who had remade the city according to his own vision—the Triborough Bridge, the FDR Drive, parks and concourses everywhere, but most particularly Jones Beach, which he designed with genius and originality. He had been a ruthless power broker but he had made the city greater than it had ever been, and Jonathan thought of him as a model. Many people joked about the second coming—'the second Moses'—but it was true that, as Moses had changed the face of the city, so had Jonathan. Only once in a generation, if that, did someone come along with the vision, the faith, and the *chutzpah* to try such a thing.

Fergus pulled the car to the stone water tower that was the landmark of Jones Beach, identifiable from miles around. There waiting was a black Lincoln Continental. Fergus and its brutal-looking chauffeur eyed each other as Jonathan waited.

In another minute or so, Messina emerged, a blunt, powerful-looking man in his forties with Roman features and expensive clothes. Jonathan followed suit.

"Mr. Broad," Messina said, extending a hand, "a pleasure."

They shook—Jonathan didn't know why. It was a preposterous gesture of gentlemanliness. But then again, he thought, maybe it wasn't so preposterous after all. Maybe it hearkened back to the origin of the gesture, in a time when men had first to show that they harbored no weapons.

"Quite a place, isn't it, Mr. Broad?" Messina said, looking out to the ocean. "One of the only places in New York City that hasn't gone to the dogs."

The wind cut right through Jonathan's thin worsted suit, but he didn't want to show how cold he was. "You didn't get me out here this time of the morning to talk about Jones Beach, did you?"

Messina smiled cordially. "I would have preferred for us to have had breakfast somewhere more congenial—I prefer the Ritz-Carlton myself—but you were difficult to reach on the phone and my business was pressing."

Messina's urbane tone was both absurd and vaguely frightening. "I prefer the Regency for breakfast myself," said Jonathan obliquely.

"To each his own, Mr. Broad."

"Now that we've done the small talk, Mr. Messina, might we get to the point of all this? I have a busy schedule today."

"I'm sure you do, Mr. Broad. All that River Park business." Messina took out a cigarette—an expensive Black Sobranie—and offered one to Jonathan. "No thank you," said Jonathan. "I don't smoke."

Messina nodded. "You take very good care of yourself, eh, Mr. Broad? I take very good care of myself too. I like myself and want to do nice things for myself."

This sort of 'Me Decade' cant sounded particularly chilling in the mobster's mouth, Jonathan thought. He glanced at Fergus, wanting to make contact.

"I admire you greatly, Mr. Broad," Messina continued. "I think you've done a great deal for this city. You know, I love this city as much as I love good food and air and beautiful women. I've lived all my life in this city and I owe it a lot. I admire what you're trying to do here."

"You didn't get me out here to draft a fan letter

either, Messina," Jonathan said, losing patience. "Get to the point."

The perimeter of Messina's smile narrowed. "I admire your plans for River Park, Mr. Broad. I think it has vision and scope."

He was beginning to sound like Paul Goldberger, the New York *Times'* architectural critic. "Thank you very much."

"I think I could be of great help to you with the project, Mr. Broad," Messina said. His breath had condensed and made the air look dirty. "I don't think you should forego my help, Mr. Broad."

"The issue of your help has already been broached to me," said Jonathan, "but frankly I don't think it would work out."

The smile remained fixed on Messina's lips. "But it must, Mr. Broad," he said. "I would be very disappointed if it did not."

It was time for bluntness, Jonathan realized. "Forget it, Messina," he said. "I'm not buying what you're selling."

"I want the restaurants in River Park," Messina said, the smile disappearing. "And the bars."

Jonathan laughed, which made Messina's face tighten dangerously. "Get smart, Broad," he said. "You don't come in with your fancy high-rises and your quiche cafes and think you own the waterfront, you know what I'm saying?"

"And you don't tell me what I do or don't do, do you hear me?" Jonathan said, feeling himself close to boiling. This cheap hood, this scum mobster, telling him what to do.

"You don't hear too good, do you, Mr. Broad?" Messina said, flexing and unflexing his fists. "You think just because you build some fancy buildings, you're on top of the world. Now listen: if we don't like what someone is doing—like someone is trying to push us out of our territory without giving us a piece of the action—then we let that person know what it means to be punished. Sometimes we hurt that person, we make that person cry. And sometimes we take someone close to that person and make that person cry.

"You have a sister, don't you?" The question hung in the air, whipped against him by the wind, and Jonathan felt a deep uneasiness invade his gut.

"What's her name? Merry?" He shrugged. "It's a funny name to give a grown-up woman, no? Your Merry like to take on five, six guys at one time? Over the course of a couple days? Give her a free tattoo, hand-made, maybe something nice like a peacock maybe, or a mermaid?"

Jonathan stared at him, feeling something he had never felt before in his life: the desire to kill. If this animal touched one hair on his sister's head, he would slice him to pieces.

"What's the matter," Messina said, "you out of words?"

"You've got enough for the two of us," Jonathan said, "and I'm getting sick of them. State your business. It's a lovely day for the beach, but I've got things to do."

Messina looked him up and down. "Tough guy, eh?" he said, with another of his chilling smiles. He reached into the car for his attaché case. Jonathan glanced at Fergus, whose face betrayed nothing but whose body was prepared. Messina turned to the driver: "Don't worry, kiddo. No violin case here. And

169

don't worry about your sister. Not yet. Now I'm just going to show you some pretty pictures."

What was he talking about? Messina must have sensed Jonathan's bewilderment, because his smile grew. "That's right, buddy. Pretty pictures of somebody we both know and love." He paused. "And have loved."

Jonathan watched as Messina's big, meaty hands worked on the clasp envelope, wondering how many people those hands had garroted, knifed, executed?

"There," he said. "One of the great natural talents of our time." Jonathan stared down at the pictures that Messina was proffering, but he made no move.

"Go on, Johnny," Messina said. "Take them."

He pushed them into Jonathan's hand. Jonathan held them for a moment, and then looked down. Flash of skin, a ruby pink wetness. A woman exposing the most private parts of herself and when he looked at the face, he felt his mind reel. Stella. How could she? It was worse than anything he could have imagined.

"Look at all of them," Messina urged.

He shook his head. Messina grabbed the pictures out of his hand. He flipped to the next one and held it up in front of Jonathan's face. The image of Stella and a dark-skinned woman buried in each other's embrace assaulted him.

"Dig this one," Messina said, his voice excited, holding up a picture of Stella in a martial helmet, with a whip and high boots and the dark-skinned woman bound and gagged.

Reflexly, Jonathan lashed out and knocked the pictures out of Messina's hand. The thug behind the wheel moved, as did Fergus, but Messina called them off. "It doesn't matter," he said. "Those are for you. I got lots of copies."

Jonathan looked down at the filthy pictures on the ground. "I don't care," he said. "I don't care what you show me."

"You think about it, babe," Messina said. "Take a couple of days. Think about how easy it'd be to have me run the restaurants and the bars, what a good job I'd do. But I warn you, Johnny, if you say no, I take these right to Bob Guccione and he prints a *Penthouse* around them and your life ain't worth squat, get it?"

"I don't give a damn, you scum," Jonathan said, his voice trembling.

Messina looked at him long and hard. "Sleep on it, buddy," he advised, and he got into his car and it pulled away.

Stella sat at a dark corner table in Le Village, a small, discreet restaurant on West 11th Street. Wayne Mullins always kept her waiting. Figuring he was using the time to make large amounts of money, she didn't usually mind, but this particular afternoon she was feeling almost crazed with the need to see him. He was the man to rescue her from all this.

She sipped at the kir, her second, and picked at a crust of bread. She had to keep herself together. When she went through periods of stress, she ate nothing. Or, more to the point, she vomited everything she did manage to eat. The pounds would just slough off of her, ten, fifteen pounds, and she would become cadaverous and pale. If that happened to her now, as it had at other points in her life, then she would be in terrible trouble. One thing she could not afford to lose, not yet at least, was her looks.

171

After she'd been sitting there for fifteen minutes, the captain approached her. Something about him disturbed her, and after a moment she realized what it was—he looked like Gabriel Messina: that same swarthy skin and too-bright smile. Anything that reminded her of Gabriel Messina was anathema to her now, and she felt her heart begin to pound in the same arhythmic patterns that had affected her last night.

"Madame?"

"Yes?" she said coldly.

"There is a problem in your arrangement? You perhaps would care to place a call?" he suggested superciliously.

She turned red. What did he think she was doing? Soliciting? "I am Mrs. Jonathan Broad," she said grandly, "and I am awaiting my luncheon companion. Are there any other questions?"

The name, as always, worked magic. He backed off with a series of obsequious bows, and returned moments later with a small plate of assorted pâtés—complimentary of course. Little did he know that the sight of these forced meats, gleaned from the pickings of rabbit and pheasant and suckling pig, were enough almost to push her over the edge.

Finally, at half past one—thirty minutes late—Wayne entered, dressed as always in faded jeans that hugged his lean legs most becomingly, a blue suede jacket, and a very fine Brown's of London shirt. He kissed her hand—he could have such divine manners when he wanted to—and begged her apology.

"I really am sorry I'm late, honey," he said, the dust of Oklahoma still coating his voice. "Something came up."

"That's okay, Wayne," she said. "Whatever."

"That's what I like about you, Stella. You're not the kind of woman a man's got always to be apologizing to. You understand the way the world works, and that's plenty rare in a woman. I feel like I share something with you—a feeling of . . . conquest."

His words put the first warm glow in her that she'd felt in days. The way he was talking . . . it was almost as if he loved her. And that word he had used—conquest—it was so right. They were good together; they were strong and powerful. Their rightness together could one day be legend.

"Let's eat," he said. "I'm starved."

She ordered the lightest thing in the house—plain broiled salmon—and she tried not to lose her lunch while Wayne went with relish at the *rognons de veau avec cèpes*—veal kidneys with wild mushrooms. The smell of it was so strong that she finally lost the battle and had to excuse herself from the table and just made it to the bathroom in time. For a long moment she sat there, feeling utterly dejected. It was the second time today she'd been sick. In the morning too. Morning sickness? She doubted it. After the two abortions she'd had years ago, it was unlikely she could get pregnant. That was another thing she had never bothered to tell Jonathan. Why should she tell men anything? It was men who got her into trouble in the first place. No, she didn't think she was pregnant. Just nerves. She needed someone to rescue her and she had the deep, gnawing feeling in her stomach that she might not find that someone.

Making her way back to the table, she saw that Wayne had gone on to the cheese course. The assemblage of chèvres and blueveined Roquefort almost made her fly off again, but she steadied herself with a cigarette and a shot of Chartreuse, drunk purely for medicinal reasons.

"Mmmnh," said Wayne, "this place is great. Got to come back here again."

He was a man of big appetites, she thought. Food, drink, cocaine, fast cars, good sex, any and all of them, in any combination. How could he condemn her? She felt sure he wouldn't abandon her in her time of need.

"Waynie," she said softly, "I need to talk to you about something."

He smiled. "You going to start in again on how we've got to take over the Broad Company? Jesus, Stel—the body isn't even cold yet."

She shook her head. "That's not it."

He smeared some Roquefort on a slice of Comice pear; she looked away. "So what is it, babe? Spit it out."

She took a deep breath; she put a hand on his thigh. "I'm in a jam, Wayne," she said. "I'm really in a terrible jam."

He kept on eating, looking at her a little more probingly now, but not saying anything, waiting for more.

"Can I tell you what it is?" she said, almost pleaded.

He didn't say yes, he didn't say no. All he did was look at her and nibble at the cheese.

She took in another deep suck of breath and then she began. "It's kind of a long story," she said, eyeing him, feeling thoroughly disconcerted by his uncharacteristic silence. "You see, years ago, when I was on my own in New York . . ."

He wasn't helping. He was silent, not even nodding. She felt a coldness and she was chilled by it. But there was no other route to travel. "I was very hungry, Wayne," she said, reaching in her bag for another cigarette. She lit up and blew smoke at the ceiling. "You know what I'm talking about, don't you?" she asked. "You weren't born with a silver spoon in your mouth, God knows. I don't have to tell you what it means to be hungry."

But he didn't say anything; he just waited. He had the master poker player's ability to keep his mouth shut.

"Someone offered me a couple of hundred to do something. I shouldn't have done it—and I wouldn't have done it if I had it to do over. But I didn't feel I had any choice . . ."

"You mean," he said, breaking the silence, "that the rent collector was at the door, your sister needed an operation, and it was Christmas?"

She stared at him.

"What are you trying to tell me, Stella?" he said, pushing away the cheese board. "You trying to tell me you turned some tricks and some old john of yours has got the goods?"

"No," she said, hating him just then. "I'm not trying to tell you that."

He grinned. "Hey, babe. Don't take it so seriously. How bad could it be?"

She felt herself relax a bit. "It's bad, Wayne," she said. "It's real bad."

"Tell me," he said, his eyes boring into her.

"I posed nude," she said bluntly.

He thought about that for a moment and then shrugged. "So? You and Joan Collins and Terry

175

Moore and Marilyn and Jill St. John and Ursula Andress and . . ."

She shook her head violently. "No," she cried. "It wasn't like that."

Again he said nothing. How could she tell him the full extent of the sordid truth?

"Maybe I don't want to hear this," he said.

She ground out the cigarette in the ashtray. His true colors were coming out, but she couldn't stop now. "These weren't tasteful, soft-focus pictures, Wayne," she told him. "This was hard-core, ugly stuff. What do they call it? Yeah. This was beaver shots. And some Lesbo action. And some bondage." His face had drawn very tight. "What's the matter?" she said. "You look shocked."

"How should I look?"

She shrugged. "I don't know. Sympathetic, maybe?"

He looked at her for a long time and then he shook his head. "I don't think so, Stella."

She couldn't believe what she was hearing. "You don't think so?" she repeated.

He wiped his mouth with the napkin and decided to forego coffee. "What are you leading up to? Somebody's blackmailing you? You need cash to buy out? Well, you're not getting help from me in that department. I don't need that kind of complication in my life, Stella. You're fun, and you're talented, but if you think I'm going to get involved in some kind of mess, then you don't know Wayne Mullins very well."

She felt her face burning. "I need your help, Wayne," she whispered urgently. "You're the only person I can turn to."

"You seem to have some very strange notions,

honey," he said. "I never offered a shoulder to cry on, understand? That's not the way I operate. I can't imagine how you figured I would." He took out a roll of bills and laid a hundred on the table. "Gotta run, honey," he said, rising.

"Don't you dare leave this . . ."

But his long, lean legs had already carried him halfway out the restaurant.

"Bastard!" she heard herself shriek, careening out of control, and then the captain was coming toward her, and she was on her feet, but he was already gone when she got outside.

She stood in the sunshine on that pleasant Village street, two mothers pushing carriages past her, a voice student singing a hymn as she headed toward school. Her life, Stella realized, had changed, just like that, in the blink of an eye. There was nobody to help her but herself. But then, she thought, that was an old story, wasn't it?

13

IT HAD BEEN a whirlwind morning. For his second breakfast at 8:00 A.M., Jonathan had met with the mayor and Deputy Mayor Daniel Potter, during which time they pledged further support to the River Park project. At 9:00, Jonathan rushed to the hospital to check in on his father, and on Merry, who was looking almost alarmingly haggard. At 9:30, there was an interviewer from *Fortune.* At 9:45, a meeting with a group of investment bankers from Lazard Frères. At 10:15, an hour of squash and trade talk at the River Club with Dave Winters of First Boston. At 11:15, a seminar with graduate students in urban planning at C.C.N.Y. At 12:30, lunch at Le Recolte with economist Morton Bender from Harvard and the senator from New York. And now, at 1:30, he was back in his office, awaiting Stella.

His busy morning in no way buried the feelings stirred up by yesterday's surreal meeting with Gabriel Messina at Jones Beach. Last night, as he closed his eyes, the images of Stella's lewdness and depravity had come rushing back at him. The idea of his having made love to such a woman sickened him. But then had they ever made love? Love was not a word that figured prominently in Stella's vocabulary.

There was a knock on the door and Lotte entered. "I brought you grapefruit juice."

"Thanks. Put some vodka in it?"

"Are you kidding?" she said. "You start drinking vodka after lunch and it's down the tubes in no time." Lotte was becoming more and more maternal these days, and he was expecting her to come in any day now with a cup of chicken soup. Actually, the idea wasn't so unappealing. At this point in his life it might be nice to have someone take care of him.

"Look at you," said Lotte. "Death warmed over. You've put on ten years in the last few weeks. Look at your hair—you're going gray and I'm not talking salt and pepper."

"Oh, come on, Lotte, give me a break," he said, downing the grapefruit juice.

"Are you taking vitamins?"

He shrugged.

She looked up at the ceiling, rolled her eyes. "Can you believe this man? I'm going out this minute to GNC to get you stress tabs. God only knows what kind of trace minerals have already leached out of your system."

"God only knows," he said deadpan, and then offered a boyish grin.

"Oh, stop it."

Suddenly, Stella appeared in the doorway. "I hope I'm not interrupting anything," she said snidely.

The grin disappeared. "Come in."

"Can I get you anything, Mrs. Broad?" Lotte asked, her dislike for the woman impossible to veil.

"Just some privacy." Stella waited for Lotte to withdraw. "Ugh," she said, sitting down, crossing her endless tan legs, and fishing in her bag for a cigarette. "Can't you send that awful woman back to the Grand Concourse or Ocean Parkway or wherever it is she hails from?"

"I don't think that's something you have to worry about," Jonathan replied. "We've got other matters to discuss."

"Ooh," she said. "That sounds serious."

"You bet it is."

She stared at him for a long while. Then she placed her hand against her breast, thinly covered by a scarlet silk Krizia blouse, and gently, almost absent-mindedly, caressed herself.

"Save it, Stella," Jonathan said. "It won't work this time."

She considered this for a moment, took a deep drag off her cigarette, blew the smoke in rings that clustered near the ceiling. "OK, what do you have to tell me?"

"I went to the beach yesterday," he began.

She gave him a quizzical look. "What's this? Burn-out?" But he didn't smile.

"No, Stella. A business meeting with a friend of yours. Gabriel Messina."

She took a deep breath, holding it for a moment. "Oh," she finally said, for lack of anything better.

"He showed me some pictures," Jonathan continued, and then waited for her reaction.

"Oh?" she said again, taking another deep drag off the cigarette.

"Funny how you never told me about that part of your past, Stella," he said.

180

She put out the cigarette. "What should I have told you, Jonathan? That I spread it for money before I met you? Is that what you think I should have done? Would you have done it?"

He smiled a little—a thin, bitter smile. "You'll forgive me, but it's kind of hard for me to project myself into that situation."

She nodded. "Yeah. It'd be hard for you to project yourself into any situation where you weren't Mr. Golden Boy. But not all of us had everything handed to us on a silver platter . . ."

"Jesus," he said, disgusted. "You're not going to start that again, are you? I thought that kind of speech went out with old Joan Crawford movies."

"I was hungry!" she cried. "You don't know what that means!"

"You're always hungry, Stella," he said.

"And what if I am?" she said, her eyes blazing. "You'd be too if you'd had what I had growing up. A father who abandoned you . . ."

"Come on, Stella. Play the violin somewhere else."

". . . and a stepfather who was screwing the pants off you as soon as he moved in, night after night, while your mother was off emptying bedpans in rich people's homes."

He was shocked. She had never told him this before. For a moment, he felt a twinge of sympathy. Obviously her childhood had been traumatic enough to warp her. "Tell that to your shrink, Stella," he said coldly. "I don't want any part of you anymore."

"What are you saying?" she demanded. "He'll go to *Penthouse* with those pictures—I know he will."

"You expect me to crawl into bed with that hoodlum and compromise everything that the Broad Company stands for just because you happened to pull down your undies for the wrong shutterbug?"

"Don't you hear me?" she cried. "He'll go to *Hustler*. You'll see those pictures on every newsstand in this city. Is that what you want?"

"I'm not worried, Stella," he said, and he meant it. "Barbara Walters'll put me on TV and I'll cry my heart out about how I was duped by a calculating and amoral bitch. You'll see—they'll be lining up to comfort me."

"I hate you," she said. "You've got ice in your veins, not blood. You don't know what it means to love anyone. You're a lousy lover . . ."

He shook his head. "I don't have time for your little tantrum," he said. "On the advice of my lawyer, I'm moving into a suite at Montague's tonight. You will be served with papers directly. You are also to divest yourself of any responsibilities concerning the Broad Company and to turn over to me any materials pertinent thereto. You will receive appropriate severance pay to see you through your transition."

She glared at him so intensely that he thought her eyes were going to pop. "Are you firing me?" she whispered.

He looked at her. "I'm getting rid of you on all fronts. As of today."

"And you think you can get away with this?" she laughed.

"I know I can. You're through, Stella."

"I'm going to drag you over the coals, Jonathan Broad. I am going to crucify you. You are going to wish you were dead when I start in on . . ."

"I said you're through. Maybe, if you're lucky," he said, with a crooked smile, "you'll have a future in a certain kind of film. But, for now, I want you out. Pack your things and clear out of this office today, or I'll have someone do it for you."

She stood up, trembling. "You're the boy who never makes mistakes, eh? Well, let me tell you something. You just made the worst mistake of your life." She turned on her heel and left the office.

Jonathan sat there for a moment, and then punched in the intercom. "Lotte?" he asked, "have you gone out yet for the stress tabs?"

Later that day, Jonathan went before the Landmarks Preservation Commission. The meeting was held at the offices of Perry Bodine, a partner in the illustrious firm of Sklar, Bodine. Present were Mr. Bodine, Esq., the art historian Winston Miles, Abigail, and Esther Esterhazy, the tremendously rich and civic-minded widow of Miklos Esterhazy, a Hungarian immigrant who had amassed a fortune in the computer business.

"So good of you to meet with us today, Jonathan," said Perry. "Just a few questions really about River Park, if you don't mind."

"Not at all," said Jonathan. Perry was one of those bumbling WASPs whose affectation smokescreened a razor-sharp mind and a pure-bred understanding of the uses of power.

"Mr. Broad," said Winston Miles, over his pince-nez, "we feel it incumbent upon us to bring to your attention the city blocks along Twelfth Avenue, whose integrity must remain untarnished." Miles was an effete who belonged in the court of Louis XV, not in New York City in the 1980s.

"Why, Mr. Miles?"

"Twelfth Avenue is an urban landscape, Mr. Broad," the popinjay said through his nose. "We can't have it tampered with."

"Twelfth Avenue is crumbling," said Jonathan firmly. "It's a playground for hookers and junkies. It's not a 'landscape,' Mr. Miles. It's an eyesore."

"What Winston is trying to say, if I may," said Abigail graciously, "is that as far as the commission goes, any plan for the city should in some way reflect the *history* of the city. The bitter lesson we've all learned is that history is not something to be addressed with a wrecking ball."

It was as if she didn't know him, thought Jonathan, as if they hadn't been together, time and time again. He smiled at her. "I think I've learned my lessons as well as any of you have. River Park will not destroy the neighborhood, but rather will enhance it."

"'Enhance' is such a pretty word, Jonathan," said Esther Esterhazy, in her thick mittel-European accent. "My late husband always used to say you can put a fancy name on something, but a gizzard is still a gizzard."

It was the kind of non sequitur that could put a stop to any meeting, and it did. Perry Bodine rushed to the rescue. "What we're saying, Jonathan, is that admirable as River Park may be, we must still cast a jaundiced eye on any project that razes rather than renovates. This is where we stand at this point in time."

"I see," said Jonathan. "Well, my friends, I'm sure we'll be able to work around that."

Jonathan was still steaming when he got to Jams, where he was having dinner with Merry. Jams was one of his favorite restaurants—he liked his food basic, grilled, and American—but tonight he had no appetite for it.

"Come on, Johnny, you're not eating," Merry said.

"I'm in no mood for it," he replied gloomily. "I feel like it's take a shot at Jonathan Broad season. First this Sherman Maloney lunatic and now the Landmarks Preservation Commission, acting like I'm Attilla the Hun, and the thought of food makes me sick."

She shook her head. "You just got through telling me this morning how I have to conserve my strength, how I can't spend day after day at Pop's bedside. Here I got all done up to have dinner with you when I would have been perfectly happy with a tuna sandwich, a hot bath, and a Hercule Poirot novel, and you're not even eating."

She reached out and put her hand over his hand. "It's not just River Park. What is it?" she said gently. "Pop?"

He nodded. "Of course. But . . ."

"But what?"

"Something else," he confessed. He looked up at her mild, pleasant face, with its unending resource of acceptance for him. "Stella and I have made the break."

Generally Merry was the essence of discretion but this time she couldn't control herself. Her face brightened as though someone had turned on a lamp behind her eyes, and she stopped just short of clapping her hands. "Oh, Jonathan," she said. "It's so right. It's so necessary."

"Merry," he said, with difficulty, "this is being done under the most strained of circumstances . . ."

"If you mean this is not going to be one of your New York–style amicable divorces, I say take what you can get."

"That's not what I mean. What I mean is that, very shortly, there may be some publicity . . . publicity of the most scurrilous kind, that's going to affect all of us."

Her pale blue eyes, which might ungenerously be described as 'milky,' narrowed. "What do you mean? Divorce is not exactly front page news these days. Hasn't been since Nelson Rockefeller found Happy."

"No, it isn't." He paused. "But a cache of porno-graphic photographs is."

He heard her deep intake of breath. "What are you saying?"

He took a sip of his wine before going on. "Stella had a . . . past. There was a time when she posed for some very unsavory photographs and these photo-graphs have now resurfaced."

Merry looked as if she were going to be ill. "But can't we . . . can't you buy them back?"

He shook his head. "That's complicated. Someone is planning on leaking them to one of the big sex magazines."

"Oh, Jonathan," she said disgustedly. "How could you have been so stupid?"

There it was, out in the open. Jonathan felt himself flush.

"I'm sorry, Johnny," she murmured. "It's not your fault. Really . . ."

"Yes, it is."

"No, don't blame yourself. We all make mistakes." She took his hand between her own thin, cool ones.

186

"Sometimes we find ourselves in love with someone we shouldn't and we can't stop ourselves and we get in deeper than we should and . . . and . . ."

She stopped herself. He stared at her. Suddenly he felt like she had secrets of her own.

"Take me home, Johnny," she said.

"Are you all right, Merry?"

She shook her head. "No, dear. I'm not feeling very well. One of my headaches—it just came over me."

He had Fergus drive her home. "Take care of yourself, Sis," he said, "and I'll speak to you tomorrow."

When he got back to his apartment, he felt paralyzingly alone. Here he was, at the top of the city, a city that he owned as much as anyone owned it, and he felt now that he had nothing. He wanted to be with someone, but who?

It came as a total surprise to him when Roxy Monahan came to mind. She made no secret of the fact that she didn't trust him, or really like him very much, but there was something about her that touched him. Unlike Stella, unlike Abigail, she was a real, unaffected, emotional woman. He had to admit that from the first he had been stirred by her flaming auburn hair and fair complexion. Hers was the kind of sexuality that didn't advertize itself with slit skirts and sheer blouses but that was a natural part of her, to be exposed gradually in the natural course of events.

It was 8:30. He wondered what she would say if he called her now, what he would say. She'd probably think he was trying to seduce her to win her over on the River Park issue. What the hell. He didn't get where he was by not taking any chances. There was something about this woman that interested him, and he wanted to get to know her better. And what he wanted, he usually got. He picked up the phone, feeling a little odd, like a high school boy calling for a date, and then forged ahead.

"Hello?"

"Hello, Roxy. It's Jonathan Broad." (Well, that was a beginning—not a brilliant one, but a beginning.)

"Yes?"

Oh boy. She was really helping things along. "I've been thinking about what you said, how I didn't really know the waterfront, and I remembered that you said you lived in Red Hook, where I've never been, and I'm feeling in kind of an exploring mood"—Jesus, she'd think he was a lunatic—"and I was wondering if I could come by. Maybe we could go for a walk, get some coffee . . ."

There was a silence on the other end. Damn it, he felt stupid. "Of course, I know it's getting late," he said, "and if you're busy . . ."

"No," she said. "That's okay. I'm just a little surprised. Sure. Stop by."

She gave him the address and they hung up. "Fergus," he said, "how well do you know Red Hook?"

"About as well as you do, sir," Fergus replied.

"Well, get out the map. We're going to 33-21 Van Brunt Street."

"This is quite a place you've got here," Jonathan said, looking out the floor-to-ceiling windows that afforded a spectacular view of the New York harbor.

"Thank you," said Roxy. "I like it."

She was dressed in old jeans and a big navy blue

and white Icelandic sweater. She hadn't an ounce of make-up on, but her skin was flawless and her blue eyes radiated a particularly incandescent sort of light.

"How long have you had the place?"

"Oh, two years, I guess." She grinned. "Two years, three months, fourteen days. This is my dreamchild, as you can probably tell." It was a loft of approximately two thousand square feet, an enormous amount of space for one person. In the middle of it was a country kitchen, with lots of pots, some copper, hanging from the ceiling, and a big old pine harvest table set with pumpkins and gourds for the season. The furniture in the living area was homely and used—she obviously was not putting money into Regency antiques. One whole wing of the loft was set up as an artist's studio.

"Do you paint?" he asked.

"A little," she said, "mostly watercolors. The harbor, seagulls . . . the usual stuff."

"That's quite a set-up for a watercolorist."

"The man I was living with was an artist." There was a pause. "That's ended, but now I rent out the studio space to an art student from Pratt. Helps cover some of the maintenance costs of this barn."

He nodded. She was, if anything, a straight shooter, right from the shoulder. He sat down in one of the hoary old Morris chairs, covered in red corduroy. "One thing though—isn't this what you call gentrification?" he asked, looking around.

She thought about that for a moment, and shook her head. "No, it's not, and I'll tell you why. I was born and bred one block from here. I've lived here all my life, and I can't imagine a circumstance, other than a stint in Washington, that would pull me away. And I'd always come back. This is where my roots are. So the fact that I choose to make a nice home in a place where I've always lived can't really be called gentrification, can it?"

He considered this and then nodded. "You're right."

"I often am," she replied. "Or hadn't you noticed?"

He grinned. "I noticed."

"So what are you doing here tonight, Mr. Broad?" she said, sitting down on the rug and pulling her knees up to her chest. "Or, to rephrase it, to what do I owe the honor of this visit?"

"I told you: I was restless. Felt like going somewhere I'd never been before . . ."

"And it boiled down to Tibet, Upper Volta, or Red Hook?"

"Something like that."

She looked at him directly. "I guess I'm a little confused. Our sessions together have not, so far, been warm and wonderful."

"I've been warm and wonderful," he replied. "You haven't."

"You don't seem like someone who comes back for punishment. At least your publicity machine doesn't represent you that way. Is that your real secret, Jonathan Broad? Are you really a glutton for punishment?"

"You're not making it very easy for me to be here tonight, Roxy."

"Oh, I'm sorry," she replied. "I didn't realize it was my job to make it easy for you to be here tonight."

His face darkened. "Maybe I should go."

"Maybe you should tell me why you're here," she countered. "Is this a date? Is this a little side action? Did you think I was going to be another notch on your gunbelt?"

He stood up. "I wanted to be here tonight because, for some very screwed up, very neurotic reason, I liked you. But it's clear it's not mutual, so why don't we just say good night."

"Let me tell you something else," she went on. "I'm not interested in married men, OK? That's not what I was put on earth for—to make their lives less onerous."

Her eyes were blazing, her complexion was high, and the red hair framed her face like a fire. "You want to know why I came here tonight?" he said. "Because I was feeling kind of low. My father's dying, I had some trouble at work I can't go into, and I felt like you might be the kind of person I could spend a little bit of time with, have a cup of coffee, talk. That's all. Strictly all." He headed toward the door. "And, it's not yet public knowledge, but my wife and I have separated, and I've instituted divorce proceedings," he added. He opened the door and headed down the steps, furious. Everything was going wrong—everything.

"Jonathan," she called from the landing. "Jonathan, wait."

He stood there for a moment, then slowly turned to face her.

"You've got to understand something about me," she said. "A lot of times I'm really sort of a jerk. Shoot my mouth off and everything. Maybe it's the Irish in me, I don't know."

191

He nodded. "Could be," he said.

"But at least whenever I realize I'm in the wrong I apologize very quickly. Will you accept it?"

"What?" he asked, not wanting to make it easy.

She grimaced. "My apology."

"Yes, I accept it."

"Good." She smiled, and he thought how beautiful it made her. "I think I'm going to take you to Lucy's."

"What's Lucy's?" he said.

"What's Lucy's?" she cried in mock astonishment. "Lucy's *is* Red Hook." She got her things together and they headed out the door. He started to walk over to the car, and she grabbed hold of him. "Are you kidding?"

He looked confused. "What's the matter?"

"If you think I'm driving up to Lucy's in a Bentley, you're crazy. I would never, *ever*, live it down."

He shrugged. "OK."

"Why don't you tell him to park it and join us?" she suggested.

He thought about the Bentley parked, unattended, on the streets of Red Hook and decided against it. Anyway, he wanted Roxy to himself. "No," he said. "Let's let Fergus do his job." They walked the block and a half, the wind from the river slicing through the streets. "You could be a thousand miles from Manhattan here," Jonathan commented.

"You're absolutely right. Most of the people here never even go into Manhattan. Most of them work in the Navy Yard or in factories in Flatbush. I'm one of the few who crosses the harbor every day."

"What do they make of you here?" he asked.

She shrugged. "I'm just Roxy. That's why I live

192

here. They don't make anything of me. They all think I'm smart, they all remember how I was class valedictorian and class president and editor of the yearbook, and they think I'd be a lot better off if I got married and had a bunch of kids like the rest of them."

"Do you have friends here?" he asked.

"Of course. Lots of them. Friendship here is different than it is in your neck of the woods. Here there's always some kind of wedding or funeral or christening or confirmation to go to. I do as much of that as I can. I like it. It's my small town, and I know everybody here."

They got to Lucy's, and Jonathan looked over the undistinctive storefront, with the ragged awning and the baby carriages parked in front of it. "This is the place," she said, with a smile. "We may see my brothers or even my father here. I hope you don't mind."

"No. I don't mind. Unless they think that we're getting to be a regular thing," he teased.

"It doesn't matter what they think," she said, leading them in.

Lucy's was crowded with old and young, mothers with children, sailors, a couple of nuns, a group around the TV watching hockey. Roxy waved to Lucy and took a seat in a corner booth. "No brothers, no fathers," she said, with something that Jonathan took for relief.

"How is it living in such proximity to your whole family?" he asked.

"It's fine," she said. "We're very close, one of those Irish clans. But a pretty screwed up one, in some ways. None of the boys has gotten married. Of course, Joe is a priest, but the others—Brendan, Dennis, Ryan—don't seem to be the marrying kind, and neither do I. Maybe it's just something that skips a generation. My mom and dad had a beautiful marriage, and maybe we all feel we're not going to get something as beautiful."

"That's kind of a cop-out, isn't it?"

She looked at him evenly. "That's quite something coming from a man who's just filed for divorce."

"I still believe in the institution," he said, "very much. And kids too—I'd like to have kids."

"Why didn't you?" she said. "Too busy with charity balls and making money and all that?"

"My wife was," he said. "She's not the maternal sort. I guess I found that out too late, although if I'd thought about it in the beginning I might have guessed as much."

Lucy came over to greet them. "Roxy, who's this?" Lucy asked, her eyes widening behind her thick harlequin glasses.

"Lucy Minciotti, Jonathan Broad," said Roxy, making introductions.

"So nice to see you," said Lucy. "Such a nice-looking young man. What can I get you two?"

"Just coffee, Luce."

"Forget about it," she said, as if the idea was too absurd for words. "Just coffee is not for young people. You'd like some nice cookies with that, I bet?" she asked, looking at Jonathan.

He looked at Roxy and smiled. "Cookies sound good."

"A smart fellow," Lucy beamed. "I'll be right back."

Roxy couldn't help laughing. "When Mom died, I was just a girl. Lucy made up her mind then and there that a young girl could not grow up in a family of five men without the help of a 'female influence.' So she took me under her wing and there I've stayed, snug as a bug, ever since. As you can tell, I don't come in here with a guy half often enough to satisfy Lucy."

Jonathan surveyed the room. All of this looked so decent and friendly and fundamental that immediately he felt better than he had in days. Maybe that's why he'd come out here.

"It looks like she did a good job," Jonathan said.

They held a look, and then she looked away. "You said something before about your father," she said.

Jonathan nodded. "He's gravely ill. Kidney failure. He's not expected to last more than a few days."

"I'm so sorry," she said. "You were very close, weren't you?"

"Probably as close as a father and son could be. It almost sounds trite to say he's my best friend, but he is. I never questioned his love and support for me."

"That's the way I feel about my family," she said. "I can show one face to the world and another to them."

Jonathan shook his head. "I can't imagine how it's going to be without him."

Lucy came over. "Pignoli cookies," she said. "Specialty of the house for my darling Roxy and her nice young friend."

"OK, Luce," said Roxy, with a sigh, "let's not lay it on with a trowel."

Lucy placed her hands on her ample hips. "What are you talking about?" she demanded.

"Nothing, Lucy. My fault," Roxy quickly mollified,

as Lucy went off in a huff. "She's touchy," Roxy explained. "Wonderful, but touchy; I'll be hearing about this for days."

"I'm sorry if I've made trouble for you," Jonathan said, smiling slightly.

She smiled back. "No trouble. All in a day's work."

They drank their coffee; they ate Lucy's splendid cookies. They talked about Stella, about disappointments in life and love, about family responsibilities, about River Park. For the first time, Roxy listened to him without defensiveness and had a sense that Jonathan's ambitions might go beyond profit or glorification.

"Listen, Jonathan," she said, "I think I have more of a sense of what you want to do with River Park. But you haven't gone far enough with it. You ought to look at a model civic project like Stuyvesant Park and get some ideas. That was a city within a city. There was room for the old, the young, families, singles. The only way River Park can possibly succeed—and I'm not even sure why I'm being so encouraging—is if you blast apart the homogeneity. Get your head out of thinking of it as a refuge for the rich and start thinking of it as a community with housing for everyone—rich, old, middle-class, working class, handicapped, you name it. You could even put a couple of tugboat slips in there."

"That's a noble thought, Roxy," he said, nibbling at the cookie. "But that's not the way New York, circa 1980s, works. Social stratification still rules."

"Listen, throw in all your yuppie stuff. Put in your ice cream shops. Who cares? As long as you've got something for everyone. Old people can enjoy sitting around fancy malls too—that's what Donald Trump found out with the Trump Tower."

"You keep talking about ice cream shops, goddamn it," Jonathan exploded. "What about everything else in my proposal?"

"Right," she said. "You've got good goodies, nice perks. The aquarium, the ice skating rink, the marina, the carousel . . . but that's the cranberry sauce, Jonathan. I'm talking about the meat and potatoes. I want to know why you don't have the guts to make this into something more than a fancy condo. I don't know why, if you're so anxious to make a mark on this world, you don't seize the opportunity to turn this into one of the real social experiments of our time."

Jonathan mulled over her words. She put out the kind of electricity that people accused him of discharging. He was excited by her. He didn't know if he agreed with her—now or ever—but he certainly couldn't ignore her. He felt the kind of release and happiness he got when he used to be at the Harvard Business School, arguing with top-rate minds on the other side of the fence.

And so they kept on arguing for what seemed like hours. Finally, Roxy looked at her watch. "Lord, look at the time," she cried. "I'm always asleep by ten. If I don't get my eight hours, I'm a witch in the morning."

"My fault," said Jonathan, as they bid good night to Lucy and walked down the street. "When things get going like this conversation tonight, I don't know when to quit."

"Don't apologize," she said, looking at him with her beautiful blue eyes. "I'm the same way." She smiled a little. "I guess we're the same in certain respects. Maybe that's why we got off on the wrong foot."

He stared at her. "No harm done," he said. "I sort of feel like we got onto some kind of even keel tonight."

She looked at him, then looked away, noticing Fergus still waiting in the Bentley outside the building. "Poor guy," she said. "What a boring job."

"It's a job," he said.

She shook her head. "I could never have people waiting on me like that. Never could have maids or chauffeurs or anyone like that around."

"You'd be surprised," he said. "Money changes you."

"That's why I'm making a point of not getting a lot of it. I like myself just the way I am—most of the time, that is."

Jonathan nodded. "I like you too," he said.

There was a moment—a long pause—and then she turned. "Good night, Jonathan," she said. "I'm glad you called."

"Good night, Roxy," he whispered as she went inside, and as he felt his unhappiness, held at bay by these last few hours with her, stream through the sluice gates.

14

GOT TO KEEP going. Got to keep going. That was the litany that went through her mind as she ran around the reservoir. Generally, she ran three miles. Today she'd run six. That was the way Stella Nevins was, she thought to herself. When the going got tough, the tough got going.

She had decided to go on the offense. She and Anderson had formulated a plan that would discredit Jonathan down to his boots. It was going to be a smear campaign—a dirty whisper campaign. Of course, no one was going to believe *her* little whispers—as of today, after lunch with Oogie, word would be out that she and Jonathan were through, that she was "Renobound" as they used to say in Earl Wilson's column—but they'd believe Anderson. He had one of those faces from which you'd believe anything. He would begin to drop hints around town that Jonathan was going down the tubes, that he was an incompetent manager, an unreliable egomaniac whose family problems were pulling him down. Anderson could get away with it; he seemed so honorable that he made Jimmy Stewart in *Mr. Smith Goes to Washington* look like Boss Tweed.

Despite Jonathan's difficulties with the project, she knew that River Park was already on a roll. Jonathan's vision—and *chutzpah*—were worth plenty, but there were plenty of other developers jumping on the bandwagon. Now everyone had become aware of the undeveloped land in that waterfront area, and everyone was scrambling for contracts. Stella was intent on positioning herself where she could catch the best trout. With the smear campaign in gear, Jonathan would be weakened, and she and Anderson could move in to swing Broad-bound contracts their way in a new company that they would set up with the singular backing of a very rich man with impeccable contacts . . . Gabriel Messina.

Her humiliation at the hands of Gabriel in his limo had been the worst night of her life, but she had learned from it. She was smart and she was tough but there was no way she was going to beat Gabriel at his own game. There was no way she was going to get out from under him. She was his, and that was it. The more she did for him, the more he'd do for her. He didn't know it yet, but she had consecrated herself to him. Today she would tell him—show him—that she was all his. And then she would do for him and do for him. She was convinced that Gabriel would jump to enter the building industry through the very legitimate front provided by herself and Anderson. Of course she and Anderson would have to discontinue their relationship, which would hardly be a devastating loss to either of them. And then, after a while, they could cut Anderson out. She was sort of fond of Andy, but lately he was blowing much too much snow up his chiseled nose.

It's amazing, she thought as she ended her run, how

exercise could drain away tensions. She was sure everything would work out for the best. The photographs would be sealed away, available only to herself and Gabriel. Maybe they would even pull them out now and again for some fun. Granted, Gabriel could be frightening, but he was still a man, and once she applied her unmitigated energy toward a man's seduction, there were very few who could refuse her. She would make love to Gabriel Messina this afternoon as he had never been made love to before. After all, they had the rest of their lives together.

Stella at Le Cirque made her way to her usual table, dressed to the nines in a big, black, incredibly dramatic Comme les Garçons jumpsuit, and a wicked, broad-shouldered purple leather Claude Montana jacket. Dark Ray-Bans covered her eyes, and in her lustrous black hair she wore an Angela Cummings clip with a diamond the size of a prune. She waved to her luncheon companion, smiled brilliantly, and as she got to the table bent down to embrace with adoration and joy the spindly figure of Oogie Banks.

"Don't you look the vision?" he marveled. "There are only three things that could make a woman look as radiant as you are: a bun in the oven; two weeks at The Golden Door; or a new man. Which is it?"

She pulled off her black leather gloves. "Order us a bottle of Roederer Cristal, Oogie. We have some celebrating to do."

"I can't bear this," he said, practically rubbing his hands with excitement. "*What* is going on?"

"Be patient, cookie," she said, in the tough manner that little fairies like Oogie found so exciting. "I've got to wet my whistle first."

The wine steward brought over the champagne and Stella made a toast. "To a new recipe for radiance," she said, and they clicked glasses and she downed the precious blond liquid as if it were Pepsi. "And, rare as it is, Oogie, you're all wrong. I do not now have—nor do I ever hope to have—a bun in my oven, as you so colloquially put it. I have not been near a spa in ages, although I wouldn't mind going. And not only do I not have a new man in my life, but I have *no* man in my life."

"What happened to our corporate raider friend?" Oogie probed, his little frog face beaded with perspiration.

"That was amusing for a while. Then it was over. *Ça va.*"

He giggled. "You are without doubt one of the great mankillers of our time, darling, right up there with Marilyn, Liz, and Lady Antonia Fraser. So what is this about being without a man in your life?"

"It's true, Oogie," she said. "I'm leaving Jonathan."

He stared at her, his eyes popping. "I haven't heard anything about it."

"You're the first in town to know," she said, gesturing for a waiter to refill her glass. "I guess by tomorrow everyone will."

Oogie leaned forward; this was a goodie. "What happened?" he breathed. "Everyone took you for a model couple, save for the occasional fling here and there."

She waited for him to light her cigarette, and took two deep drags. "Can I speak to you in confidence, Oogie? As a friend?"

"Of course, darling," he said, patting her hand. "What did the brute do to you?"

202

"Jonathan is a very sick man," she said, chewing her lower lip. "He's managed to alienate everyone in his firm. Living with him these past six months has been a nightmare. You can't imagine. The insomnia, the drinking, the . . . I guess you'd call them anxiety attacks, where he becomes alternately immobilized and abusive. And now, with his father's condition pretty much hopeless, I really think he's heading for a major breakdown." She covered her face with her hands, then went on as though through superhuman effort. "He beat me, Oogie. And not just once."

"Oh, come on, Stella," he said, playing with a breadstick. "Beating you would be like taking on a puma barehanded."

"I'm telling you the truth, Oogie. I've never told this to anyone before. He'd go at me with a hairbrush. He'd throw lighted matches at me . . ."

Oogie giggled. "Pussycat, please. I haven't seen this scene since Lana Turner and Ross Hunter got together."

"Oogie, stop it!" she hissed, bursting into tears that drew glances from everyone around her. This was grand-scale stuff, but the bold gesture was called for. "This is no time for jokes," she said, choking back tears, fully aware that this was only the first of many performances in which she would have to prove herself the consummate actress she had always considered herself. "I've been living through something very horrible. Please don't be arch about it."

He gave her a probing look, lifting up her chin to examine her more closely, "You *are* serious, aren't you?" he said, shocked.

"It happens in Milwaukee, it happens in Detroit, it happens in Houston, it happens in San Jose. And it

happens in the Broad Palace, Oogie. Can you understand what I'm saying? Jonathan Broad has been
unraveling at the seams, and I've done everything in
my power to help him stay together, but I can't any
longer. Am I wrong to want to protect myself, Oogie?
Please, tell me I'm not wrong."

His puffy eyelids fluttered in surprise. "Of course
you're not wrong, dear. My poor Stella. What you've
been through. Now you just let Oogie help you. If you
need a lawyer, money, anything—you let Oogie help
you."

"All I need, Oogie," she said, looking at him with
astonishingly sincere eyes, "is your friendship."

She raced the plum Lamborghini down the Long
Island Expressway. She cut in and out of lanes in
control of the wheel and the highway. Nothing could
stop her.

Her life, she sensed with an enormous feeling of
power and excitement, was getting back in shape. She
had come up against some big curves in the last few
weeks but they weren't too big for her to handle. She
was a survivor.

She plugged in a Talking Heads tape and put it up
to full volume. She felt good. She felt good! After sex
and money, revenge was one of life's sweeter gifts.

She pulled off the highway at the Shelter Rock Road
exit and headed toward Kings Point. It was amazing
how confident she felt, heading into the lush estate
area called Kings Point, and to the greenest, lushest
part that was the province of her new love, Mr.
Gabriel Messina.

As she had the other day, she announced herself

over the intercom and then sailed through the gate. I can buy him and sell him, she heard Gabriel boast. That kind of power had an effect on her, and she felt all warm and excited as she neared the entrance.

The little butler—Indonesian or Indian or whatever —admitted her with a gracious bow that she took in stride, and she headed into the library. There was Gabriel, and this time he looked up. "Hey, babe," he said. He was watching "The Little House on the Prairie" on TV. "Ever catch this show? It makes you cry."

"Remind you of your own family?" she said sassily, and he looked at her even more carefully and smiled a little. "Funny."

She sat down and pulled off her gloves. She could make a show of it, if she wanted, and she wanted. She had beautiful hands and feet—she had modeled brief- ly for Jergens lotion a long time ago. "Have I told you what a beautiful place you've got, Gabriel?" she said pleasantly.

"No," he said, flicking off his favorite show. "I don't think you got around to it last time actually."

"Actually, I didn't," she said, playing with him. "But it *is*. Those roses in that vase—are they from your garden?"

He shrugged. "Who knows?"

"You should know, Gabriel," she said, looking hard at him. "You should familiarize yourself with the better things in life."

He stood up and walked to where she was sitting; he stood over her, emphasizing his supremacy. "Looks like you're gonna be a national celebrity in a few days, Stella," he said.

She smiled slightly, even though she felt within as tightly wound as a rubber band. "Tell me about it, Gabe," she said, caressing his name.

He looked hard at her, trying to figure her out. "The pictures," he said bluntly. "I'm handing them over to Bob Guccione. I think he'll handle them with a little taste—I want to do that much for you, Stella, for old time's sake."

"That's sweet, Gabe. But what happened? You couldn't strike a deal with Jonathan?" she said, forcing herself to be calm.

He shook his head. "The guy doesn't seem to care if his wife shows beaver in a national magazine. Can you figure that?"

She drew out a cigarette, lit it, langorously blew smoke at the ceiling. "So now you know what I've been living with," she said.

"Yeah. Well, the money must've helped."

She shrugged. "You yourself said you could buy and sell him. Between you and me, Gabe, he's in a crunch. His credit rating is in serious trouble. The kind of deficit financing he's into leads nowhere but down."

Gabriel watched her, waiting for more.

"I'm leaving him, Gabe," she said. "I've had enough."

He smiled, and the smile led into a laugh that grew and grew. She sat there, waiting for him to be finished, and it took a while. "That's rich, Stella," he said. "Your husband just learns that his wife is a minor-league smut queen and *you're* leaving *him*."

Got to keep going. Got to keep going. "Sometimes you need an external force to help you make a decision," she said. "I'm not worried about the pictures, Gabe. You can't worry about the past, about what you did when you were a hungry, stupid kid. I hope people will understand, but if they don't, they don't. All I know is that I have you and the late lamented Jerry Castriata to be grateful to. You helped me make a decision that had to be made."

"That's great, Stella," he said, sitting down opposite her, "but where does that leave me?"

She put out her cigarette. "You, Gabe? What can I say? I couldn't keep up my end of the deal so you get to do whatever you want with the pictures. I figure Guccione will give you some good money for them."

He shook his head. "You don't think I really want to see those pictures published, Stella, do you?"

She smiled—a little more broadly this time. She was measuring out every nuance as though she were Garbo and the camera were enlarging and capturing her for posterity. "You could have fooled me," she said slyly.

"I was trying to strike a deal," he said. "You were the bargaining chip. It wasn't that I wanted to personally hurt you . . ."

"So what was that action in the car the other night?" she said.

He shrugged and gave her a sheepish grin. "I just wanted you to know to take me seriously."

"Gabe," she said, with a slight tease in her voice, "would I ever take you less than seriously? That's why I'm here today. Listen, do what you want with the pictures. But I wanted to make you a proposition."

"You got to watch out for that, sweetie. You could get arrested for that."

She let out a rich peal of laughter. "That's good, Gabe. You're cute . . . when you want to be. Now here's the story. As I told you, Jonathan's been deteriorating rapidly. His father's illness—or should I say his father's imminent death—has been a crippling blow. There's always been a really pathological dependence on the part of Jonathan and his sister on the father—and now Jonathan's paying the piper."

"Spare me the psychiatric background, OK?" Gabriel snorted. "Get to the point."

"The point is that the Broad Company is about to go into a tailspin. I'm leaving, and Anderson Kendall has given me his every assurance that he would join me in a new venture."

"Congratulations. But what's an Anderson Kendall?" Gabriel responded.

She giggled. "An Anderson Kendall is second—or third, depending on how you look at it—in command of the Broad Company, with total knowledge and access to trade secrets, a Harvard background, impeccable social connections, and a pipeline to major backing."

"Sounds good. Why's he in your camp? You laying him?"

She pouted. "Don't be crude, Gabe. And why do you always think the worst of me?"

"What worst? I'm thinking about your best."

"Anderson and I have a purely professional relationship," she said. "I don't put my shoes under anyone's bed, Gabie."

"Hey, Stella," he said. "That makes me warm all over."

"All over?" she replied, arching an eyebrow.

She saw him watch her more closely. Got to keep going. Got to keep going. She shook her tousled mane of hair. "I think you could help us, Gabie. I think we could help you. Before long, Jonathan's contracts will jump ship like rats smelling the end. And we can be there to pick them up as they swim to shore. We can make River Park ours, Gabe—this is the time to move in on him."

He looked at her long and hard. "I don't know why—call it a sixth sense—but I have my qualms about getting into bed with you."

She let that sit for a moment, then she rose, slowly and deliberately, and went to sit next to him. "You shouldn't ever have qualms about that, Gabe," she murmured.

There was another moment—everything in the rich, plush room hung still, waiting for the turn of events—and then he reached out and touched her cheek with his big hand. She covered his hand with her own hand, and then she drew his hand against her lips and then, with a touch like a whisper, she licked first one finger, then the other. She felt a shudder from him, and a bubble of happiness burst within her.

"Maybe," he said, his voice strangely thick with feeling or desire, "we were meant to be together."

"We were," she crooned. "We were."

"We have something special," he said. "Don't we?"

She touched him where he was big. "Oh yes," she whispered. "We have something special."

He wrapped her hair around his hand. "What could be wrong?" he said. "You like all the same things I do—money, sex, sex, and money. We'd be great business partners. What the hell—let's do it. If you can bring down Jonathan Broad's house of cards, I say let's do it."

"Oh, baby," she groaned. "Let's seal that with a kiss."

She pressed her lips against his; the kiss was prolonged, probing, as they passed their flow back and forth to each other. He took her in his arms, started to undress her, but she slithered out of his grasp, stood, reached out for him. "Not here," she said. "I want a bed. A big brass bed. I want all the room in the world."

He grinned and stood and followed her as she led him up the stairs. Got to keep going. Got to keep going. She felt pumped up, good, and fine as she mounted the steps. She was an athlete running the race, the big race.

As she stood at the top of the steps, she seemed to know just where to turn. She held his hand and directed him. She went into a big room with a big brass bed—just as she'd known it would be—and dark curtains on the window. Only an ape like him would have dark curtains closing off the harbor view. She led him to the bed, sat him down, straddled him, worked her tongue against his, undid the buttons on his shirt, worked her tongue against his full brown nipples and he was groaning and she liked that groaning. Got to keep going got to keep going. Pulling off the lilac leather jacket. Undoing the mysterious buckles and catches that held together the black, blousy jumpsuit that hid the absolute symmetry and voluptuousness of her curves. Then she was before him in her black lace lingerie and slowly, slowly she peeled it off and she was naked and she swayed rhythmically back and forth in a kind of mating dance that no man could refuse. After a while she reached down and found him all swollen and hard and she helped him off with his things as if she were a geisha and he was a lord and he liked it, he liked it, and she thought how he would never be cruel to her again, how he could never think, for a moment, that he could live without her because no one knew how to touch him the way she did.

She kneeled before him and did everything he wanted and some things he didn't even know he wanted until she showed them to him. Again and again, she stemmed his tide, grasping him hard to prevent his finishing this exquisite, tortuous pleasure, and when he was almost weeping with forestalled joy she pushed him back on the bed and mounted him, all warm and wet and she rode him wildly, telling him in harsh guttural thrilling tones how he should service her and finally, when he could stand no more, she let him come and she joined him in howls that made him come again, the first time it had ever happened to him that way but not, if she could help it, the last. He was hers, she realized, hers forever, as she kept on riding him, telling herself over and over and over again in the haze of the orgasm she hadn't even expected to have but that was there as a bonus that she had to keep going, had to keep going.

15

ON THE EIGHTH day of his coma, David Broad opened his eyes. He looked around the room and saw his daughter sitting on a chair nearby. He was in a bed, and he was in a hospital. "What are you doing?" he called. She put down the magazine she was reading, stared at him with an expression that expressed alarm, disbelief, and something like hysteria, and then burst into tears. "Pop!" she cried. "Pop!"

Jonathan was in a meeting with Tom Duncan, a senior vice president of Con Edison, when Lotte came running in. "Excuse me," she cried, "but it's about your father, Jonathan. Wonderful news!"

He made sure that Fergus beat the world-record time up to Mount Sinai. He raced through the corridors, bounding up the stairs when the elevators weren't immediately forthcoming. And he charged into the room to see this man he loved so dearly, this man who had just returned from the land of the dead. "Pop!" he cried.

They embraced each other. Merry joined the embrace. The family was together.

The doctors had no explanation. It was a miracle,

and they cautioned, one that might not last. Jonathan was amazed at how lucid his father was. His father was an amazing man, the world an amazing place. That afternoon, when he left, he declared a holiday for himself. He felt, for the first time in weeks, truly vigorous and happy . . . and horny. He thought of Roxy, it had been a few days since he'd seen her, and his feelings about her were complicated. If there was to be a future with her—and he profoundly hoped there was—it would have to be tackled carefully. But today was not the day for caution, and he decided Abigail Forester was just what the doctor ordered. He rang her up, found her at home, and got himself invited over.

He gave Fergus the afternoon off and walked the few blocks from Mount Sinai to Abigail's town house. Roseanna, the Mexican maid, greeted him with her usual suggestive smile. He grinned back, wanting her, wanting everything all at once. "Thank you, Roseanna," Abigail said, intercepting them as she came down the stairs. "Come into the drawing room, Jonathan," she suggested.

She poured them each a sherry and sat down next to him. The sunlight poured through the French windows at just the right angle. The yellow damask upholstery shimmered. The walnut paneling glowed. The forced bulbs in cachepots and jardinieres spread their color and perfume. Abigail, in a Fair Isle sweater, gray flannel slacks, and her blond hair held back by a velvet headband, looked the essence of ripened, mature beauty. Everything was just right until she opened her mouth. "I'm glad you happened to call, Jonathan. I was going to call you. I just wanted to be the one to tell you that the Landmarks Preservation Commission has decided to come down rather heavily against River Park," she announced bluntly.

He looked blankly at her. "What are you talking about?"

"As you know, Winston Miles has taken serious exception to your plans. He points to the precious resource of 19th-century waterfront urban housing and has announced that he plans to do everything in his power to protect it. I thought it incumbent upon me to tell you that he has quite thoroughly swayed the commission in his favor," she said, gazing coolly at him.

"Surely you don't feel that way, Abigail," he said.

"I'm afraid I do, Jonathan. My husband's family has ties to that neighborhood, you know. My husband's paternal grandmother established a settlement house there in 1903. I can't sit by and see that piece of history torn down and cast away."

"That's utter crap," Jonathan protested. "I've maintained from the first that I intend to protect everything that deserves to be protected and that I would honor the commission's advice and guidance in doing so. But I'm sure you'd agree that the Commission cannot expect to preserve every two-bit waterfront hovel that should have been torn down decades ago."

She frowned at a hangnail and then at him. "You're missing the point."

"And what is the point?"

"That you're going too fast, Jonathan," she said, with a flicker of contempt. "That's the point."

What was she saying? That he was an upstart? Her face had a remote expression. She was letting him

214

know that their relationship had little effect on her "ethics" and her commitment to the commission. "Whose side are you on anyway?" he demanded.

"I'm on the side of the commission, of course," she said in her clenched-jaw finishing school accent. "I thought you understood that."

"No. I didn't understand that," he said angrily. "I thought we had some kind of relationship. I didn't realize that I was just stud service for you."

He glared at her. "Then let Professor Miles stick it to you," he said furiously.

"As a matter of fact he does," she replied, with a frigidly sweet smile, "and very nicely too. And, furthermore, that's precisely the kind of remark that won't get you anywhere. As I said, Jonathan, you're trying to proceed much too quickly."

What she was telling him was that he was a parvenu, scrambling up the ladder too fast, too perilously, not paying the right kind of homage to the power structure of this city. That he was the grandson of a Dutch plasterer and he shouldn't try to go places he wasn't invited. Well, she could screw herself, he thought angrily—or let the professor do it. He certainly wasn't going to, ever again. "I can see myself out."

"It's no bother," she said, making as if to rise.

"No," he insisted as he headed for the door.

"Jonathan," she called. "I hope this hasn't incurred hard feelings. None of us on the commission are insensible to the many ways in which you have already improved the quality of life in this city."

"That's touching, Abigail," he said tightly. "Thank you."

He closed the drawing room door behind him, and

headed toward the door. "Goodbye, Mr. Broad," called Roseanna. He turned around to where she stood by the door.

"Have you forgotten something?" she said, a coquettish smile spreading across her lips.

"Have I?" he replied.

"I think so," she said, in her gentle tones. A thin, delicately shaped hand went decorously to her breast.

As he moved across the elegant foyer, her smile disappeared, leaving her lips parted.

"How could I forget?" he said, as he reached her, his voice husky. He bent down to kiss her, and she responded with a passion that had been too long pent up.

"Come," she said, taking his hand, leading him down the back steps into the kitchen, "I know a good place."

She took him into a dark little pantry and locked the door. Quickly, deftly, she slipped off her uniform and stood before him in tawny nakedness. She began to undo her hair, and he reached out to help her, then bent to take her nipples in his mouth as she moaned softly. Quickly he lowered his pants and presented himself hard and full to her sweet caresses. He figured she didn't have many opportunities here, with one day a week off, and he was intent on leaving her with a memory of pleasure.

"Oh, sir," she groaned, as he fondled her until she was beside herself, "stop."

When he saw how ready she was, he lifted her atop him and in the close, musky pantry, smelling of dried sage and clove, he drew in and out of her with measured, silent, deliberate strokes, and she bit into his neck so that she wouldn't cry out, but finally she did, in little broken cries, as he grunted and filled her with his desire.

"Will you be coming again soon?" she asked, as they dressed.

"I don't expect so," he said frankly. "I'm sorry."

"Then I won't be seeing you again?" she asked, her liquid brown eyes imploring him.

He felt guilty, having used her like this. In the past, he had always allowed his desire to run rampant. Now he felt that it wasn't right, it wasn't fair. He wanted something else with a woman, even though what he had just had with this woman was so sweet and so satisfying.

"I don't think so," he said gently, touching her cheek. He withdrew his wallet and gave her one of his cards. "Come see me," he said. "If you have a problem—need a job or some money—I'll help you."

Her sad face brightened with a tentative smile. He leaned down and kissed her tenderly—and finally—and then headed out of Abigail's house, a quizzical smile on this face.

In the afternoon he went to his gym, knocking himself into the kind of shape that he wanted to be in, recapturing the feeling of energy and purpose which had been dissipated in the last few weeks. Pablo, his trainer, remarked on the tension in the muscles and devised some special exercises to stretch him. After that, there was a rubdown and a sauna and a nap. When he awoke to some iced herbal tea and a light snack of apples, grapes, and Armenian string cheese, he felt better than he had in ages, in spite of his talk with Abigail.

The whole time in the gym, he was thinking about

his conversation with Roxy. Maybe she was right. Maybe when he had first conceived River Park, he thought of it as "big" in only the most superficial meaning of the word. Why couldn't it be bigger? Why couldn't it be a sort of city within a city? He already knew that he could build the richest and most glittering of buildings—Broad Palace proved that. Perhaps now it was time for the sort of "social experiment" she was talking about.

Getting back to his office, he called a meeting for tomorrow with Anderson and Sidney and his architect Wilson Marriner. Start thinking about a new kind of River Park, he would instruct them. Sidney, of course, would burst a gasket and Anderson would look quizzical and Wilson would look pained, but he would tell them what he wanted. A River Park with housing for everyone. Goddamn it, maybe Sherman Maloney was right! He looked at someone like Stella, whose whole life was money, and he asked himself if that's what he wanted. Did he want to be a man of vision, like Robert Moses, who could really transform entire decaying blocks of this city into something valuable for everyone? He could have the glitz— Roxy's idea of an aquarium stuck in his mind since the one in Coney Island was no great shakes—but he also had to think of reality, and reality meant the middle-class and families and children and the poor and the old and the handicapped. He suddenly felt as though he were at a crossroads. With his father's miraculous recovery and the separation from Stella and the discovery of Roxy, Jonathan felt almost reborn.

He was so fired up that he decided to call Roxy. He hadn't spoken to her after that night, and he wasn't altogether sure why. Maybe he felt as if she wouldn't, in the end, take him seriously enough, and maybe he couldn't face that.

"Roxy Monahan," she said as she picked up.

"Is this the deputy commissioner for the waterfront?"

"Yes, it is. Who is this?" she said impatiently.

"It's Jonathan, Roxy," he said, a little disappointed she hadn't recognized his voice and his silly joke.

"Oh. Jonathan. Hi."

Oh. Jonathan. Hi. He'd been hoping for more. Like "where have you been, I'm dying to see you." He took a deep breath. "I'm calling to invite you out to dinner, tonight, if possible. Now give me a second: I wouldn't think of taking you to Chanterelle or the Quilted Giraffe or Lutèce or any of those places I might take a more base and avaricious sort of person. I had in mind a little hole-in-the-wall place that a Taiwanese diplomat once took me to in Chinatown. And no chauffeur, we take cabs just like regular people. How about it?"

There was a silence. "I'm awfully busy," she said.

"Please, Roxy. I don't handle rejection well. It almost never happens to me," he said, making sport of himself.

She laughed—it seemed she couldn't help it. "OK, Jonathan. How can I resist seeing you as a 'regular' person? I figure I can clear out of here around seven. Pick me up then?"

"I'll be there," he said.

He reported back to the office in the late afternoon to catch up on some phone calls. Lotte gave him a hard examining look. "You look like you turned a corner," she said.

He agreed. "Life's looking a lot sweeter all of a sudden, Lotte."

Before he went downtown, he had Fergus whisk him up to Mount Sinai again. David, sitting up in bed, looked like a new man. It was astonishing to think that only twelve hours ago he had seemed near death. "Welcome back, Pop," Jonathan said. "You look splendid."

"Splendid I don't look," David said. "Alive I look. I sent your sister home. She was worrying over me and hovering over me and making me so nervous I couldn't stand it. The nurses told me she's been living by my bedside. You shouldn't let her do that, Jonathan."

"You're right, Pop. I've tried to get her to go home and rest and all that, but she wouldn't."

"So what do you have to tell me, Johnny? How's business? How's life?"

Jonathan's eyes filled with tears. It was so amazing to be sitting here like this, talking to his father this way. "Problems, Pop. Problems and solutions." He wondered if he should tell him about the divorce proceedings, but decided nothing too taxing was the order of the day. In another moment, the nurse came in to tell him that it was time for his father's nap and that the visiting time was over. Jonathan kissed his father goodbye. "Welcome back, Pop," he said again.

An hour later, Fergus dropped him off a few blocks from Court Street. He decided to live dangerously tonight—no bodyguard. He walked the few blocks and found Roxy waiting for him downstairs. "Hi," she said. "You made it here without your limo, huh?"

He nodded. "Wasn't so hard," he said. "It's amazing how well one can do with taxis."

"Isn't it?" she said.

They grabbed a cab and headed over to Division Street. On the way, Jonathan told her about his father. "Oh, Jonathan," she said, "that's incredible. It really sounds like a miracle."

She was a miracle, he thought, as he looked at her profile. Maybe Stella was more conventionally beautiful, certainly Abigail was more classically so, but right now neither of them held a candle to Roxy Monahan; her face was intelligent, alive, and passionate. You felt she really cared about things—about causes and people and ideas. "It *is* a miracle," he agreed. "And I feel very, very grateful."

When they got to the restaurant, the owner made a big fuss over them, the sort of thing she usually hated but in this instance it was so friendly rather than obsequious that she resisted the impulse to bolt. It also meant that they got the most wonderful Chinese food she had ever eaten, going at a whole steamed flounder that was so fresh it might have swum onto the plate. "What's it like, Jonathan?" she asked. "Everywhere you go, you get the best food, the best wine, the best seats . . ."

"That part of being rich and famous is very nice," he said honestly. "It's pleasant not to have to wait on lines, not to have to be treated badly at the hands of haughty maitre d's and petty bureaucrats."

"Present company excluded, that is."

He looked at her with intense interest. "Somehow I don't think of you as a petty bureaucrat, Roxy."

"That's not what you said the first time we met. The first time we met, you, in fact, called me a bureaucrat."

"No, I didn't."

"You sure as hell did, Jonathan." She laughed a little, but then got serious. "Jonathan, I've been thinking about you a lot, and the fact is I like you a lot more than I expected to."

"Well, that's a start . . ."

"No, let me finish," she said, holding up a hand. "I like you a lot, but I've still got my job to do. My job is protecting the waterfront, and as long as I continue to see River Park as a threat to it—and I do—I don't think we should be seeing each other."

He listened to her and then he nodded. "You're right, Roxy. And I'm glad you have the integrity to say that. Not that I questioned your integrity for a minute," he added, with a grin. "But the fact is that I think you're going to stop thinking of River Park as a threat to the waterfront. The fact is you've opened my eyes to a lot of issues. Not just you, but also Sherman Maloney and even the Landmarks Preservation Commission, even though I think most of the latter are full of shit."

She looked at him quizically. "I'm not sure I get it, Jonathan."

"All along I've been thinking of River Park and proposing it as the best and the brightest of all the other condos I've put up around town. And yes, you were right, what I had in mind was essentially a playground for the rich. But the other day, when you talked about Stuyvesant Park, I guess it sort of turned my head around. I have nothing to show you yet, Roxy, but I've called a staff meeting for tomorrow and by the end of the week I will have a whole new River Park plan on the boards. I want mixed-income housing, I want community space, I want waterfront facilities. I want to integrate River Park into an existing community."

She looked at him as though she were trying to gauge his honesty, and when she decided that she found it there, she smiled. "That's good to hear," she said quietly.

All the way on the cab ride back to Red Hook, he told her about his new plans for River Park. He'd seen a park for the handicapped in Oslo that had made a great impression on him, and he had in mind a cluster of special playgrounds.

"There's no telling where we could go with this," he said excitedly. "Imagine River Park food co-ops, River Park day-care centers . . ."

She couldn't help laughing. "It's not hard to figure out why you're as successful as you are, Jonathan. You take a ball and really run with it."

When the cab pulled up to her loft building, she began to say good night, and he couldn't help interrupting her. "I don't want to say good night yet, Roxy. Do we have to?"

"Well, it *is* late . . ."

"We're still young. And if a woman doesn't invite me up for coffee at the end of a date, I feel lousy."

She smiled. "OK, bud. Come up for coffee."

She wound up making tea for them, orange spice with lots of honey and ground cloves. They sipped it at the long harvest table, with a recording of Chopin's waltzes on in the background. It was funny, he thought. He was an attractive man with a clear sense of his own sexual power, and he couldn't even begin to remember all the flight attendants and socialites and secretaries and Mexican maids he'd slept with.

But now he was really puzzled by just the right way to reach out and touch this beautiful woman whom he wanted more than anything in the world.

"Roxy," he said, "I've got a question for you."

"What?" she asked, after a moment's hesitation.

"I know you're the deputy commissioner of the waterfront and I'm the fat-cat builder, but do you think we might have a future together?"

She seemed to mull it over for a moment. "I suppose we should find out," she said finally.

Just reach out, he told himself. Reach out and touch her. He caressed her hair, then her cheek. "Roxy," he said. It was different from other times. All his confidence—his bravado—it wasn't there. She seemed to sense this and met him halfway. And then they came closer together.

"We're looking for trouble," she murmured.

"No," he said, as he kissed her neck, her hair.

"Big trouble."

"We can handle it, Roxy."

"OK," she said, as she kissed him deeply. "But don't blame me if we're making a mistake."

It wasn't a mistake. It was one of the best experiences he had ever had in his entire life. With Stella, in the beginning, it had been a technicolor fantasy of unbridled lust, with all parts working, all parts go. But with Roxy, it was altogether different. The lovemaking, as passionate as it was, had also a sweetness to it, a tenderness. It was altogether very strange—very strange and wonderful. Everything was so new, every aspect of each other to be discovered so astonishingly original and longing, and yet it was as though they had known each other all their lives. There was a basic trust between them, and something called affection. He had the uncanny, disturbing, elating, and shocking sense that he was already in love.

As always, he awoke before dawn. Tiptoeing out of bed he went to work putting up the coffee, scrambling some eggs. His activity—and the cooking smells—got her up before seven. She padded to the big pine table in a plaid wool Kreeger & Sons nightshirt, her mane of red hair in glorious disarray. "Are you always up this early?" she moaned.

"Yep."

"Would you mind if I asked you why?"

He laughed. "Just my chemistry."

She went over to where he was standing and put her arms around him, hugging him tight. "You're going to have to change your chemistry, bud."

"For you, Roxy, I'll change my chemistry, my biology, my physics . . . you name it."

They kissed and, in that kiss, there was the slightly peculiar, slightly exhilarating feeling of knowing that it was working just as well the morning after. "Scrambled eggs?" he said.

"I hate eggs," she replied bluntly. "Come back to bed. We have a half an hour before we have to go."

He hated to see food go to waste, but considering the alternative . . .

By eight o'clock, they were at Lucy's, getting some more hot coffee, looking like lovers for all the world to see, and who cared? When she saw her brothers and her father, she waved them over and asked if they remembered Jonathan and they said of course they did and no one seemed to mind that they were together in a new and obviously different way.

As usual Roxy rode on the *Galway Bay* over to

Manhattan, but with Jonathan along the trip felt very different. The silver glint of the skyscrapers in the morning light, the boom and whistle of traffic on the harbor waters, were now heightened so that it seemed as if she were seeing things for the first time. Jonathan, too, was transfixed by the spectacle and together they stood on the stern of the boat and felt the sea spray in their faces, cold, bracing, salty.

"You see, Jonathan?" she said, talking to him not as an adversary but as a lover with real, hard questions. "You see why I don't want this changed?"

He nodded. He put her hand to his lips and kissed it tenderly. "I'll protect everything you love, Roxy. Believe me. I swear it."

He held her close as the tug pulled toward its berth, delivering him to the city that he had once been fool enough to think he could possess.

He fairly sprinted into the court of the Broad Palace. Like a boy in the city for the first time, he looked up the soaring atrium, at the wall of water that flowed into the moat crossed by a series of beautiful Carrara marble bridges and he thought to himself, I made all this. He'd had that feeling before, but today was different. Today he was less interested in being a superman and more interested in being a human being connected to other human beings.

Arriving in the office, he found everyone looking considerably less lively—less *alive*—than he was. He felt like jumping on a desk and screaming, This is life, folks! Welcome to it! If his life were a musical comedy —and maybe one day his *would* be a musical comedy —this would be the big song and dance number at the end of Act One.

"Hi, Sidney! Hi, Lotte!" He waved as he went into his office. The incredible view hit him and he felt, more than ever, at the top of the world.

"Coffee!" he called to his secretary. "And some of your fine Sara Lee danish, if you please."

As she came into his office she had a strange look on her face. "You weren't home this morning, Jonathan," she said.

He made his hand into a gun, aimed it at her, and fired. "Right you are, Lots."

"Jonathan," Lotte said, "we needed to reach you this morning . . ."

"Hey, Lotte," said Jonathan, with a laugh, "what do you want from me? I've got a life to live, you know." He shook his head. "Man, I sure could use that coffee."

With great deliberateness, Lotte walked over to his desk, and suddenly he knew something was very wrong. He didn't think he wanted to hear it, whatever it was. No, he was sure he didn't want to hear it.

"I'm sorry, Jonathan . . ."

"Lotte, the coffee . . ."

She had tears in her eyes, and she reached out to put her hand on his shoulder. "Your father, Jonathan . . ."

"He's great. I saw him last night. It's a miracle . . ."

"He died, Jonathan," she said, the tears welling up.

He shook his head. "Lotte, I saw him last night. That's not funny."

"He's dead, Jonathan. 7:13 this morning. It was a massive stroke. I'm so sorry, baby. I'm so very sorry."

He stared at her and slowly, very slowly, the understanding came. "They say it happens that way sometimes," she murmured, but he didn't hear another word she said. Already he was very far away, in a strange place he had thought he wouldn't have to visit for a long time still. He wondered how he would make his way back.

DAVID BROAD'S FUNERAL brought out everyone of importance in the city of New York: the governor, the mayor, both senators, three congressmen, several Federal judges, the deputy mayor, the borough presidents, the city councilmen, the state senators, many of the nation's most famous investment bankers and chief operating officers, along with assorted glitterati who were friends of Jonathan's, all assembled in the Church of the Heavenly Rest on 90th and Fifth, a Gothic cathedral that seemed surely grand enough for the occasion. As eulogies praised David as a model of fairness, sobriety, and substance, Jonathan and Merry sat holding hands, lost in their own thoughts. To Jonathan, the occasion had a dreamlike quality. He simply could not believe his father was dead.

To the haunting strains of the *Adagio for Strings*, Jonathan and Merry left the service. Merry suddenly reached out to grip her brother's arm. "Don't look," she said, "but there's your lovely wife."

Indeed, there stood Stella in modish black, offering a fine impersonation of bereavement. With her usual sense of purpose, she approached them. They began to walk away, but Stella was quick and put a restraining arm on Jonathan. "I'm sorry," she said. In her black matte jersey dress, she looked as sleek and fit as a panther. Jonathan stared at her, and then managed to pull away from her, turning toward the waiting car. "I just hope you two will survive this," Stella called after them.

"That awful woman," Merry whispered. "I think she's really a witch."

As they neared the car, he looked behind him and she was gone. In her place, he noticed, with a sense of elation that it was necessary to disguise, was Roxy. *I always see my friends,* he heard her say, *at weddings and christenings and funerals.* She was smiling at him, the warmest, gentlest smile that existed in this world. His heart ached, for it was too early for them to be seen in public together, and yet he fervently wished that he could have her arms around him now, comforting him as he felt the full weight of his loss.

In the car, Merry sat silently for a long time, but then, with a new sense of purpose he hadn't expected of her, she spoke. "I feel so strange," she said. "Papa's dead and it's just you and me. Suddenly, Jonathan, I feel more free than I've ever felt before."

He was frankly shocked by her words and she could tell. "I've never been a happy person, Jonathan," she said, with a heavy sigh. "I think you know that. My whole life has been marked by fears, insecurities, depression. I've seen so many therapists, tried to get help in so many different places." She looked up at him. "You didn't know that about me, did you, brother?"

He shook his head. "Why did you feel you had to keep it a secret?"

"I'm full of secrets, Jonathan," she whispered, "but I can't tell you about them. Not just yet."

The interment at the cemetery was strictly private —only Jonathan and Merry and a few close relatives. That was the way that David would have wanted it. As the coffin was lowered into the gaping hole in the earth, the clods of dirt raining upon it, Jonathan felt himself plunging into something like a state of shock. He began to weep, unabashedly and unreservedly, as Merry stood by him, dry-eyed and tightly holding his hand. "We're on our own now, Johnny," she said, as they headed back to the car.

He nodded gravely.

In the car on the way back to Manhattan, they sat without talking, listening to Schumann's Spring Symphony, one of David's favorite pieces of music. They went back to their father's apartment, where Merry made omelets for them and insisted that he eat. He did as she said and, he had to admit, felt better for having someone to take care of him.

"Merry," he said, later that night, "why didn't you cry?"

She looked at him and then shrugged. "I don't know, Jonathan. I suppose I wasn't ready to let go."

"What are you holding in?" he demanded, wanting the truth.

She stared at him. "Do you really want to know?"

"Yes!"

She reached into her bag, withdrew a cigarette, and lit up. "I didn't know you were smoking," he said, trying to keep the reproachfulness out of his voice.

"I told you," she said gently, "there's a lot about me you don't know."

"Yes," he said. "So I see."

She took a deep breath. "How about some cognac?" she said, obviously nervous.

"OK."

She poured two snifters and went to sit down next to him on the plush yellow sofa. "All my life, Johnny, there's been a war going on inside me between the good girl and the bad girl. I've only let you and Pop see the good girl part of me. But there's more."

He had the sinking feeling that she was going to tell him something very bad. He couldn't bear to hear it—not today.

"You see, Johnny, all my life I've been angry. Very, very angry. It started when you came along . . ."

"Merry . . ."

"No. Wait. Hear me out," she said. "You see, girls never counted for very much in our family. It was a boy—*you*—that mattered. And I was cast aside. I guess when I realized what was happening, I refused to be the good girl and go along with it. Oh, I'd *act* like the good girl, but I'd keep the bad girl alive inside of me."

"Merry, this sounds like some kind of psychoanalytical . . ."

"That's exactly what it is, Jonathan, and don't say bullshit," she said fiercely.

He looked at her, kept his mouth shut, let her continue.

"The problem was I didn't quite know how to be the bad girl," she said with a rueful smile. "For the longest time, I thought I'd be in love with you, Johnny—in love with you in the wrong way—and that would serve the purpose," she said, reaching out to touch his arm.

He recoiled from her touch. His deepest, most

censored suspicions about her were not unfounded, he realized with a sickening feeling.

"Now, now, brother," Merry said with an ironic smile. "I stopped that. Really. I decided it was low-percentage. No returns in it. So I went looking for something else bad to do, and I found it, at school, with the other girls."

He didn't know what she was talking about.

"You're not saying anything," she said, puffing on her cigarette. "You're not helping."

"I don't understand," he said feebly.

"Oh, no?" she said, arching an eyebrow. She took another puff and stabbed out the cigarette. "I became a lover of women."

He looked at her as if he were seeing her for the first time. Now it was making sense; now it was coming together. All along, deep down, he had felt that there was something not quite right about her, and now he knew what it was. His sister was a lesbian. He didn't know what to say—he didn't know what he felt. All he knew was that he had better say the right thing. "Is this what you want?" he asked.

"Yes," she said, pleased. "It's what I want. I started out feeling that I wanted to do something bad and this was the bad thing I found to do, but then I found out something more significant, Jonathan. What I was doing wasn't bad. It was good—good for me. After years of therapy, I can accept what I am. I can finally accept the fact that I cannot achieve the kind of intimacy with a man that I can with a woman."

He nodded.

She reached out and took his hand. "Johnny," she said, "even though I spent so much time in my life hating you, I love you very much. You've got to believe that. I guess I can't help it," she laughed. "You're good and you're loving and I want you to be happy. I think I'm happy now, Johnny—I'm finally happy—and I want the same for you."

He nodded again, out of words.

"I'm going to stick around long enough for you to get on your feet, Johnny," she said, "and then I'm going away for a while."

"Where?" he demanded, feeling as if he were dodging bombshell after bombshell.

"There's a woman, Johnny—a special friend of mine—who owns a design firm in Paris. She wants me to join her there, to be her partner. It's what I want, Johnny. I'm a rich woman with no responsibilities, and I want to take some chances now. But I also want to see you through this."

He looked at her for a long moment. It suddenly struck him that this sister of his—the mouse, as he used to think of her—was really a very brave woman. He put his hand on top of her hand. "Merry," he said, 'I don't know if I understand or can absorb everything you've told me today, but I promise you—I'll try."

"I knew you would, Johnny," she whispered.

They sat there, in silence, for a long time, as he reflected on the way his life was unraveling and confronted the empty feeling that was draining through him.

In the weeks that followed David's death, Jonathan fell into a depression from which he could not emerge. Despite the ministering of Merry and Lotte, he moved around like a ghost. He spent more and more time at the gym, sitting in the hot tub, floating.

"Is this what you think Pop would have wanted to leave behind as a legacy?" Merry demanded, barging into the gym one afternoon. "A filleted fish named Jonathan Broad, wallowing in warm water?"

"I'm sorry, Merry," he said distantly. "You feel liberated—freed to do whatever it is you want. I feel different. Maybe it's called grief."

"Maybe it's called the first time in your life you've never had Pop there to watch his beaming boy," she said bluntly. She saw him wince and softened her tone. "I'm sorry, Jonathan. Seeing you like this—it's just no good."

Roxy, too, addressed his black mood. Over dinner at the River Cafe with its sparkling view of Manhattan, she watched him pick at the lobster *américaine* and decided that she, too, had had enough of his self-indulgence.

"Look at you, bud," she said, shaking her head. "A mere shadow of your former self. Do you know how criminal it is to pick at *lobster?"* she said archly, trying to temper her words.

"Please, Roxy," he said. "Don't you get on my back too."

"What's the matter?" she said. "Everyone persecuting you?"

"Goddamn it, Roxy!" he snapped. "Lay off!"

She put down her cutlery and applauded. "A show of anger—a sign of life—hooray!"

He ran a hand through the shock of graying hair, attractively incongruous with his still-boyish looks. "Don't I get a chance to lick my wounds a little?" he said. "Or do all of you think I should just keep going, without a look back, as if nothing's happened?"

"Jonathan," she said, "you've had a very heavy loss. We understand that. But it's getting time to move on with it."

"Who the hell says? You? Merry? Lotte?" he exploded. "I'll move on when I'm good and ready!"

"And what about River Park? What about everything you decided you were going to do there? The grand 'social experiment' you were going to undertake? You're going to put that on hold because you've suffered a loss?" Roxy countered.

"Yes! OK? Yes! I am putting River Park on hold! What about it?"

She gave a rueful little laugh. "If anyone told me six months ago that I'd be sitting here boostering River Park, I'd have told them to get their heads examined."

"Well maybe the tables have turned," Jonathan said. "Maybe River Park doesn't seem quite so important to me now."

"I don't understand that," she replied. "I just don't. Do you think you're the first person to suffer a loss?"

He stared at her coldly and then rose, throwing down his napkin. "Thanks for your sympathy, Roxy. Fergus will take you home," he said. "Good night."

"Jonathan!" she called after him, as he walked out of the restaurant, but he didn't turn around.

Anderson and Stella celebrated at Le Zinc, the chic bar in Lower Manhattan.

"To us!" Stella toasted, raising her glass of Roederer Cristal.

"To us," Anderson concurred, with a touch of reluctance Stella opted to ignore. She took a long draught and then gave a satisfied sigh. "Dear Jonathan," she laughed. "Could anyone ask for more cooperation?" she said. "Here we are, going around town smearing our boy, concocting rumors about the deep slide he's on, and what do you know? He lives up to it like a man."

"Frankly, I'm a little surprised," Anderson said. "I knew he'd take David's death hard, but not as hard as all this."

"He's weak," she said contemptuously. "He's never had to really fight for anything in his life. Oh, he's had to do his share of sports—jousting, feinting, parrying. But he's never really had to fight! Now Daddy's gone and John-Boy folds. Who's he going to be the best and the brightest for? Who's ever going to care as much as Daddy did?"

"I guess you know your man," Anderson said.

"Listen, babe," Stella replied. "Right now, as we sit and rub footsies, Gabriel is putting pressure on some of the higher mucky-mucks around town to throw the contracts for waterfront development toward the River View Corporation. By the way, you like the name?"

"Stunningly original," Anderson said with a wry grin.

"Screw original," she said. "We're going to come in with bids that will make Jonathan's plan look like amateur hour."

"Good for you. So," he said, with strained enthusiasm, "when do you want me to come over?"

"In a few more weeks. Your job now is to do as much damage to the Broad Company from inside as you can."

Despite his efforts to the contrary, Anderson's expression sagged slightly.

"What's the matter?" she said.

He shook his head. "Nothing."

"Nothing, my ass. You're not getting an attack of guilt, are you, Andy?" she said with a crooked smile. "Not you. Let's face it—conscience is not your long suit, honey—don't pretend it is for my benefit."

"I don't know," he said. "For a moment, I was remembering what it was like to trust someone."

"Trust me, baby," she said. "Trust mama."

He reached out to run a finger along her well-made ankle. "OK, 'Mama.'"

"Now don't be naughty," she cautioned. "We're through with that. I'm a one-man woman now, remember?"

He laughed. "You? A one-man woman? Not since Catherine the Great has there been a less persuasive advertisement for monogamy."

She shrugged. "You can't have your cake and eat it too," she said, mischievously squeezing his thigh. "Anyway, we shouldn't be mixing business with pleasure." She rose and gave him a peck on the cheek. "Talk to you tomorrow, luv. Keep those sweet little ears of yours open and that dear little tongue of yours working its dirty business. Everything is going aces. Before the month's out, Jonathan Broad will be gone and forgotten."

It was on a Wednesday afternoon that all hell broke loose within the Broad Company. A friend of a friend of Sidney Farrell's reported back to him that Anderson Kendall had said some very strange and off-putting things to him about Jonathan Broad. Sidney reported this and Jonathan, casting out a wide net of feelers, learned that Anderson and Stella had been seen together around town in the last few months. It didn't take Jonathan long to put two and two together. He had Lotte get together a hefty cash amount and then he called Anderson into his office.

"Anderson," said Jonathan expansively, the heavy blanket of his depression lifting for the moment, "sit down, please. Coffee? Tea?"

Anderson gave Jonathan his million-dollar smile. "Jonathan, you know I steer clear of caffeine. It's poison."

"Yes," said Jonathan. "You take very good care of yourself."

Anderson's smile stayed intact, but his dimples diminished ever so slightly. "Are Wilson's sketches in yet for the aquarium?" he asked.

Jonathan had put the aquarium high up on Wilson's priority list. It was just the kind of civic gesture that could help put River Park across. Wilson, of course, had grumbled mightily in his patrician way—"I've no feeling for fish," he had intoned—but Jonathan had pressed him on it. "Yes, would you like to see them?"

"Of course," said Anderson enthusiastically.

"Of course," Jonathan returned.

The two men stared at each other. The naturally ruddy color began to drain from Anderson's face.

"Why do you do it Andy?" Jonathan whispered.

"What do you mean, Jonathan?" Anderson said. "I don't quite understand what . . ."

"Let's not bother with all that. OK? Give me some credit. It may have taken me longer than it should have to find out what you've been up to but the truth's out now. Don't try to make an idiot of me and please don't make one of yourself."

Silence reigned in the splendid office. The sun

streamed through the brass blinds, casting a golden light on the proceedings that was beautifully inappropriate. "Why?" Jonathan repeated. "Tell me—was it money? I would have given you money. Credit, titles —whatever you asked for. So what was it?"

Anderson's jaw tightened. "Opportunity knocked, Jonathan," he said, resolved now to come clean. "It seemed the right thing to do."

"The 'right' thing?" Jonathan said, throwing the word back in his face. " 'Right' by what moral standard, Anderson? Certainly none that I know."

Anderson said nothing, staring straight ahead.

"Stella was behind this, wasn't she?" Jonathan said, shouting now. "How did she get to you, Andy? How did she turn your head, my friend? My friend who was there with me at my father's bedside—showing me what friendship was all about, you bastard!"

Anderson squeezed the bridge of his aristocratic nose, looking down.

"Look at me!" Jonathan demanded.

Anderson looked up. His expression was suddenly weary. "What do you want me to do, Jonathan?"

What could he say? He had been betrayed and it was bitter. With a decisive gesture, he set the briefcase on his desk and opened it. "Your money, Andy," he said quietly. "Take it and get out."

"Jonathan . . ."

"I said get out," Jonathan repeated.

He watched Anderson snap the briefcase closed, his handsome face now filled with hot blood. Jonathan buzzed Lotte and she sent in a security guard, at whose appearance Anderson paled. "He'll see you to the door," Jonathan said.

"Jonathan, let me just say that . . ."

"Your time is up," Jonathan said with finality, turning his back to him.

Alone in his office, Jonathan stared the future in the face. Jonathan had not fully assessed the psychic damage that Stella and Anderson had done to him, but he knew the wounds were deep. With a self-knowledge he had never really had to utilize before, Jonathan realized he was at a crossroads. He could feel sorry for himself, or he could fight. He sat there, staring out at the view, contemplating the city he loved more than anything in the world, and made his decision.

"He knows," Anderson told her, calling from a phone booth in the Regency Hotel. "Jonathan knows."

Stella sat quietly in her dressing room, the walls lacquered Chinese red, the ceiling painted in filigree, and she began to weigh her contingencies.

"I'm out," said Anderson. "Albeit with a nice piece of cash in hand—Jonathan has class that way. I'll tell you—but I can't be walking the streets for long, Stella. The shelf life of a fired executive without a good alibi is about two days."

Somehow, somewhere he had bungled it, Stella thought, and so he was of limited use to her now. Certainly his contacts could prove helpful, but did they really need him? She had begun to feel that he too was weak: a pretty boy, who wanted everything to go his way, but who had no real resources to back him up. When word got out of his skullduggery, he'd be more a hindrance than a help.

"Sit tight, Andy," she said softly. "We'll take care of you."

"You damned well better," he cried. "You talked me into this harebrained scheme and made me . . ."

"I made you do nothing," she said flintily. "Now pull yourself together and stop being a crybaby."

There was a silence on the other end of the phone. She looked at herself in the mirror, suspecting a clogged pore on her chin. "I've got to go," she said. "Call me tomorrow. I'll let you know what's up."

She hung up the phone. Perhaps it was all to the best this way. Anderson and Gabriel were hardly a match made in heaven. Light and dark, night and day—it wouldn't have worked out. She decided that Anderson would get on Gabe's nerves and she didn't want to let that happen, not to Gabe and certainly not to Andy. She didn't want to see Andy get hurt. She didn't dislike him—all he needed was a kick in the ass and he was getting it, and he'd have the rest of his life to lick his wounds and get it up again.

She looked at the mirror and put the mascara brush against her tongue. She licked it and then applied the mascara to her eyes. Fascinated with her face, she brought her features—her eyes, her sensual lips, her prominent cheekbones—into high relief, and watched herself become a different person. She could become anything she wanted to be, she thought, as she put on the eyeliner. She could do anything she wanted to do. Then why was she having so much trouble?

In a piercing moment of clarity, she saw the end of her trouble. She knew now what she wanted to do. She wanted Jonathan dead. Why hadn't she thought of it before? she asked herself, as she put on the coral lip gloss that made her lips look like the petals of some rare flower that grew only in hot places, like the bases of volcanoes or the bellies of great green jungles. It would all be much easier that way. Gabriel had showed her how easy it could be, the way he had helped her out with Fat Jerry. She would speak to Gabriel about Jonathan. She was sure he would agree.

That night, Gabriel told her she had never looked more beautiful. He was taking her to dinner tonight at a private club. From the outside, the unmarked brownstone in the West Thirties looked utterly undistinguished, even shabby, but inside it was done to a turn. The taste was very much toward heavy carmine draperies, gilt, and pink marble, but the expense was apparent everywhere. Gabriel had arranged a dinner for her and his guests, two "businessmen" from the Southwest, in a private room. She'd anticipated her decorative role and was dressed for it in a scarlet taffeta gown, her best diamonds, and $1200 scarlet alligator evening slippers with solid gold heels from Roger Vivier. In her hair was a gardenia. During dinner, her reflection in the smoky oval mirror took her own breath away. When the talk drifted toward "business," she excused herself and spent time in the billiards room. She shot a mean game.

When his guests left, Gabriel took her up to one of the private salons on the top floor where a bar was stocked with every imaginable kind of liquor and liqueur, cognac, and brandy. She asked for Remy Martin, he put on a recording of Plácido Domingo and Montserrat Caballé in *Tosca,* and they sat on one of the two plush velvet settees. "You like?" he asked.

"Of course," she said. "It's lovely. Did it used to be a brothel?"

He laughed with sheer delight. "It still is a brothel. I can be the john and you can be my lady of the night."

Lady of the night. Yes. It was right. Now she remembered; now it all came back to her. He bored quickly and he liked to play games. Some of his games had proved too kinky for her the first time around. But now she had grown up. Nothing was too kinky for her. Somebody famous—Franklin Roosevelt? Jimmy Durante?—said "I abhor nothing human." She felt exactly the same way. Anything two people did together was fine with her. There was no such thing as sin. Her mother, a converted Catholic, had taken them every Sunday to a service where the idea of sin had been drummed into her. Even as a child, Stella had kept her resistance in place, under her tongue, waiting to bite down on it, to release the poison pleasure all through her system. Now, as an adult, she knew that if you didn't play along you lost, and nothing—no sin in the world—was nearly as bad for you as losing.

"You like to play games," she said. "That's good," she murmured.

He looked at her with a tender smile, something she had never really seen from him before. She wanted him to trust her as he trusted no one else in the world. "Play any game you want with me," she whispered, reaching out to caress him. "I'm your toy."

Slowly, almost hypnotically, he removed his tie. She took his cue and, reaching behind her, she began to undo her fastenings. "No," he said, putting a hand on her hand. She looked at him questioningly, encouragingly. The success of a woman such as herself had everything to do with anticipation. She sat on the settee, her coral lips slightly parted, sweetly awaiting him, and felt a pulse of satisfaction as he brought his lips to hers. She had done well. She had anticipated.

As they kissed, she felt something wrap itself around her neck and tighten. Her eyes shot open to see the most horrifying expression she had ever seen. Blood lust, his eyes hooded like a lizard's. His tie was around her neck and growing tighter. She pushed at him, kicked hard, but it only got tighter. "No," she heard him say, "no," and she clawed at him and kicked him as he said "no" until finally she realized he was giving her an instruction. Panic beat through every part of her, but she made her mind keep working and she stopped struggling and closed her eyes and let him lower her to the floor. She let him do what he wanted, and when he was spent, he rolled off of her.

When she was sure that he was in a deep sleep, she sat up and reached for her dress to cover herself. Reflexly she began to shudder, but then she made herself stop. She could live with this, she thought. It was only a game. If she played the game, then she might win, and if she won, he would do anything for her and she would have whatever it was she wanted.

Roxy was in her kitchen making pea soup when the doorbell rang. She wasn't expecting anyone and felt the inevitable moment of uneasiness that any single woman in New York feels at the prospect of an unexpected visitor, but she wiped her hands on the dish towel and went to the door.

"Who is it?" she asked.

"Flower delivery."

She looked through the peephole and decided it looked kosher. She opened the door and was presented with an enormous object covered with kelly green tissue paper.

"Sign here, lady."

She did as she was told, and when she tipped the boy and he went on his way, she took the package over to the harvest table and began undoing it. To her astonishment and delight, it was a great big basket—obviously an antique of great value—filled to the brim with wildflowers. She found the card and read it.

"Dearest," it said, "I knew you'd be pissed with me if I sent you something as elitist as roses. Just a little something to celebrate my return to the living."

It was the sweetest thing anyone had ever done for her, and she ran to the phone.

"You really liked them?" he asked, his tone pure pleasure. "They were picked this morning upstate."

"Jonathan, they're beautiful. And I'm so glad," she said, a broad smile on her face, "that you've come back to life."

He came later that evening to her loft and filled her in on everything that had been happening. "How could Kendall have done that to you?" she cried, outraged.

"He fell for Stella," said Jonathan. "I can't blame him a hundred per cent—the same thing happened to me."

"Well, what's the outlook, Jonathan?" she asked. "What's going to happen?"

"It's pretty bad," Jonathan admitted. "The whole time I was spacing out, Sidney was trying to clue me in. Not that he knew the real story, but he was sensing out there, with his contacts in the PDC and the mayor's office and the banks, that a real resistance to the Broad Company was affecting the River Park project. The poison was injected pretty deeply, it seems, and I wasn't listening to a word of it."

"Go on," she said, wanting the whole story.

"We've also found out that Stella has stolen Broad Company specs and been fed privileged Broad Company information. She's set up a corporation called River View, no less, and is positioning herself to present rival bids on the waterfront development. And believe me, her bids are going to be low."

"But she has no credence . . ."

"She has Gabriel Messina behind her," he said bluntly.

"Messina? The organized crime figure?" said Roxy.

"I don't mean Messina the greengrocer."

"Break the story to the *Times,* Jonathan," she counseled. "Expose River View for what it is—a front and nothing more."

"We have no evidence of that, Roxy. They're not stupid. All their money is laundered."

"Listen, Jonathan," she said setting her jaw, "they still have to get past the Waterfront Commission. From what you tell me, they're not going to have a prayer."

"We can't count on that, Roxy. Messina's got a lot of friends in high places."

"Well, I'm in a high place and he's not going to get past me," she said.

He reached out to tousle her hair. "Big Shot," he said. "You think there's any way I'm going to let you get involved with Gabriel Messina and his friend Stella?"

"Don't patronize me, Jonathan," she said. "If what you tell me is true I have a responsibility to see it through. It's my job and it has nothing to do with my feelings about you."

"Are you telling me you can put aside your feelings about me?" he said.

She looked at him and smiled. "I may not be able to put them aside, but I can separate them out."

They kissed. "I've got to say, I like having you on my side," Jonathan told her.

"I like being there," she whispered.

The next morning they fueled up at Lucy's and took the *Galway Bay* across the Manhattan.

"So what are you going to do, mate?" asked Roxy's father, who had been told the whole story.

"I'm just trying to figure that out," said Jonathan.

"You got to fight dirty," said Brendan, drinking coffee that looked like diesel oil. "When you fight a dirty fighter, you got to fight back dirty yourself."

Jonathan weighed Brendan's words. He certainly could think of the dirty ammunition to use against Stella: the pornographic pictures—if he could get a hold of those negatives, he could pass them along to the right party and run her out of town. But could he really do that? He questioned whether he had the stomach for that kind of mudslinging. And if he didn't, was he in the wrong game in the wrong town?

"When you play dirty, you're left with dirt on your face, Brendan," said Roxy firmly. "You can't come away clean when you play dirty and it would be a Pyrrhic victory if Jonathan won the fight by discrediting himself and his own values."

"Real noble, sister," said the acerbic Brendan, "but it's not quite the way the real world works."

Jonathan tuned out of the discussion. He walked to the stern of the *Galway Bay,* cruising along Buttermilk Channel, coming closer to the island of Manhattan. Every time he saw that skyline—whether it be by boat or plane or helicopter—he still felt infused by the same sense of boyish wonder he'd always reserved for it. It was a spectacular city. None of the familiar encomiums did it justice—a *wonderful town, top of the heap, the Big Apple.* They couldn't begin to capture the majesty of it, the drive, the fantastic pulsating engine that this city was. He had been in all the great cities of the world—London, Paris, Rome,

249

Berlin, Tokyo, Shanghai, Bombay, Rio, Moscow—
and although all of them had their particular aspects
of greatness, in his mind none of them measured up to
New York. Paris was more beautiful and London
more gracious and Rome more ancient but New York
was a definition of urbanity. As accused as he had
always been of being a marauder, Jonathan now
realized that his destiny, in this time and this place,
was to be a protector. He would not let Stella and the
thugs win this one. He would see River Park go up,
and, God willing, he would see the way it changed the
face of the city and the temper of people's lives.

He went back to Roxy. "I'm calling a press conference today," he told her. "I don't have plans yet, but
I'm going to operate on bravado and adrenalin. I'm
going to uncover the new River Park—mixed-income
housing, community space—all the aspects of this
'social experiment' we've thought up. And Stella is
going to be left in the dust."

She digested this for a moment and then nodded
sagely. "Get Sherman Maloney up on the podium
with you," she advised.

He grinned. 'You've got smarts," he said. "You're
going to go places."

"Yeah," she said offhandedly. "Peck Slip. We're
docking in three minutes."

Several dozen reporters from both the print and
visual media were assembled in the lot on Twelfth
Avenue and 53rd Street, one of the many parcels that
Jonathan had bought up when he first conceived River
Park. Jonathan decided it was a good place to have the
press conference, realizing that the atrium of Broad
Palace would have been far too grand.

Around him were his people—the faithful ones—Sidney and Lotte and the dour but indispensable architect Wilson Marriner and Merry. He glanced at Merry and she gave him the thumbs-up sign. He smiled back, feeling closer to her now than he ever had, which surprised him. But the new Merry that had emerged was a far more immediate, giving person than the one who had been replaced and Jonathan was more than ready for her.

Sharing the spotlight with Jonathan was Sherman Maloney, dressed in a decent blue suit for the occasion. And running shoes. He wasn't going to give up his iconoclasm for no one, nohow. He had brought with him scores of his people—the faithful ones—and there was an excitement in the air.

"Members of the Press," Jonathan began, "I asked you here today because I have something I want you to see."

He nodded to Wilson, who removed the cloth from the glass case containing a model of the new River Park proposal. The reporters—and the crowd—inched closer.

"The Broad Company has revised the River Park concept," Jonathan announced. "Mr. Maloney has done an inestimable job of organizing the community and bringing to our attention the housing needs that must be met. I am now committing housing units to each and every community member who stands to be displaced by River Park."

A buzz broke out—startled, suspicious, cynical, excited.

"Empty promises!" someone from the audience shouted out, causing the buzz to inch up a few notches in volume.

"Mr. Broad," called out Curt Peters from local ABC, "are you actually proposing subsidized housing for this site?"

"I am proposing mixed-income housing. Low-income—middle-income—upper income," Jonathan replied.

"How are you going to attract the upper-income-brackets under those conditions. Mr. Broad?"asked Alexandra Donald of the *Wall Street Journal.*

Jonathan smiled. "In order to answer that very sensible question, I suggest we turn to our model."

Wilson Marriner and Jonathan proceeded to point out the new special features of River Park, which included reasonably priced underground parking; a ferryboat down to the Wall Street area; marina facilities; and, of course, Jonathan's pet aquarium.

"Mr. Maloney," asked Lukas Dodd of the *Times,* habitually one of Jonathan's most severe critics, "do you really trust what's happening?"

The crowd of spectators came to a hush as they awaited their leader's dictum. Maloney looked around, taking his time, sucking on his sourball. "You know, I've been around crooks all my life," he said in his sandpaper-and-vinegar voice. "Forty years I sat in court listening to every four-flusher and scam artist trying to pull the wool over people's eyes. After forty years, I think I can say I got a pretty reliable b.s. detector built inside of me. By now Broad and I have spent enough time together for me to go on record as saying I believe this guy. Maybe I'm going to wind up with egg on my face, but, damn it, I believe him."

He and Jonathan faced each other. Jonathan extended his hand; Sherman Maloney shook it. The flashbulbs popped. Yes, it would make great copy,

Jonathan thought, and it would take the wind out of Stella's sails, but there was more to the moment than that. With a real sense of destiny, Jonathan had the feeling he was turning a corner in his life.

In the ensuing days, as his public-relations machine cranked out stories about the "social experiment" of River Park and how, as a social blueprint, it would rescue the city from gentrification, the media paid even more attention to Jonathan than he had ever enjoyed before. Of course there were also the editorials that cast a jaundiced eye on the transformation of "Mr. Palace" into "Mr. People," but even Jonathan had to admit that a little cynicism was a healthy thing.

"Look at this," said Lotte, reading an article from *Newsday,* "they got you pegged as a regular Robin Hood."

"You say something, Little John?" Jonathan called, cupping his ear.

"I think the direction I've always really wanted to go in, even if I didn't realize it for so long," he told Roxy over dinner in her loft, "is politics. I've made the money—I know I can do it. I know when it comes to putting a deal together, nobody's better. But I want more than that. I look at people like Bob Geldof, who could put together the whole "We are the World" thing, and I ask myself why can't I do that? If I'm so damned good at moving and shaking, why can't I move and shake for something bigger than the biggest goddamned building in the world?"

"Oh my God," said Roxy, in mock horror. "I've created a Frankenstein."

Slowly, he put down his fork and rose from his seat. Menacingly—monstrously—he lumbered toward her.

She shrieked and he jumped her. And they played monstrous games.

The next afternoon, Roxy attended the opening ceremonies for the Palisades Hotel, the newest addition to the line of Broad Hotels. The entire time she was there, as she watched him move through the crowds, she thought about what Jonathan had told her the day before, and she believed everything he had said. She was convinced that his ambitions really would take him into something bigger and better than what he had been doing thus far. He was a man of extraordinary energy, direction, accomplishment, and persuasion. If he put his mind to a future in politics, there's no telling how far he could go. As she watched him, it occurred to her that she must have been wearing The Look, that look of rapt attention and pure devotion that Nancy always had for Ronnie. Was this mastery of The Look part of her future? She couldn't even think about it. In the tumult of these last weeks, she hadn't found the time to contemplate their future together.

She looked around. The grand ballroom, done in shades of ecru and moss green with a Regency feel, was quite perfect. Indeed, the entire hotel—an elegant limestone box seventeen stories high—would indisputably become a prominent addition to the city's list of hostelries. A good half of the rooms had spectacular river views; the two dining rooms were magnificently appointed and ruled by the finest chefs; and the entire enterprise already had the spankingly efficient aspect of a crack European operation. Jonathan paid his hotel managers top dollar, and they were worth it. The Broad Hotels were already synonymous with flawless service. She wondered how much Stella had to do with all this, and how the hotels would fare without her effective, if unpleasant, management of them.

The festivities for the new hotel were tasteful, colorful, and good fun. There was a fashion show; there was entertainment provided by some of New York's finest cabaret talents; and there were welcoming speeches by the Swiss-born manager, Gustav Dieter, and now by Jonathan himself. Jonathan's greetings were warm, direct, and engaging. He was a proficient speaker, thought Roxy, able to connect immediately with an audience. It was a talent that would serve him well if his plans for the future panned out.

And of course, there was Peter Duchin and his orchestra and some good old-fashioned ballroom dancing. As Jonathan moved across the dance floor to take her hand, Roxy thought he was the handsomest man she had ever known. Oh yes, there were little things wrong with him—one eye was slightly larger than the other, and his bottom teeth had remained crooked despite all the money that could have bought all the orthodontics he needed, and there was that shock of silver hair, his most distinctive feature, which he had had since the age of twenty-two and which she loved but perhaps not everyone did. Still, as far as she was concerned, she would change nothing.

"May I have this dance?" he asked, as he approached her. They danced to the strains of Irving Berlin's classic "Change Partners," and she felt as good and warm and safe as she could ever hope to feel. "We're going to have to talk, you know, about the future," he murmured into her ear.

255

"Not just now, OK bud?" she murmured.

"Come on," he said. "I'm a young man on the go. I've got my whole life to plan out . . ."

"Mr. Eager Beaver," she smirked.

"I would like to do something very naughty to you right now on this dance floor in full view of . . ."

But suddenly he stopped. She felt him tense up. "What is it?" she said. She saw him staring at something behind her and she turned to see Stella, resplendent in a black Chanel suit with yards and yards of gold chain. "What's she doing here?"

"That's what I'd like to know," he said, through clenched teeth. "But whatever it is, it's over. She's leaving. Right now."

"Jonathan, don't make a scene. It isn't worth it. This will be over in ten more minutes."

"Maybe you're right," he said. They continued to dance. Stella, in the company of a handsome Hispanic man, took the dance floor and maneuvered herself over. "Good of you to invite me, Jonathan," she said, "after all the effort I put into this hotel . . ."

"I'll always be eternally grateful to you," he shot back.

"You should be." She evaluated Roxy. "Who's Red here?"

"Shut up," Jonathan muttered. "You're pushing your luck."

Flashbulbs popped, recording the meeting which would no doubt be emblazoned on the pages of *WWD* and *Interview,* a good joke for the whole city. Jonathan felt his anger growing. As the music came to an end, he and Stella looked at each other, the antipathy between them so thick you could cut it with a knife.

Then Jonathan turned. "Let's go, Roxy, we have guests to greet."

He'd found a good-looking woman, Stella had to admit, even if she was dressed like she'd just walked out of Gimbel's.

"Do you wish to make this dance?" asked her escort, a Filipino diplomat named Jorge Romero.

She shrugged. The band went into a waltz— *Wunderbar.* "Why not?" she said.

It was good that she'd come. No one would have thought she'd have the nerve. Her nerve should never be underestimated. As she watched Jonathan move around the room, she realized that she felt nothing for him.

At one-thirty, Duchin thanked his audience and bid them farewell. Jonathan took the microphone to thank everyone for coming, then positioned himself by the front entrance, right outside the revolving door, shaking hands as people left.

"Beautiful job, Jonathan," said Elsa Davis, a well-known Broadway actress. "I can't wait to have a romantic tryst here."

"With anyone I know?"

She laughed and leaned over to pinch his cheek. "Naughty, naughty. But give me a ring any time."

Roxy watched from a distance. It was almost time for her to go back to work—she had to make an appearance in court this afternoon—but she enjoyed watching Jonathan's style. Even the way so many women draped themselves over him did not really disturb her.

"Fabulous, Jonathan," said Suzy, the social columnist. "It's new and beautiful and smart. It reminds me of a great Left Bank hotel."

"Come again," he said. "Any time."

As Roxy watched, she became aware of an older man with a grayish complexion, thick glasses and closely cropped gray hair waiting in line to shake Jonathan's hand. His clothes had once been very fine, but despite careful maintenance, they were really, now that she looked more closely, on their last legs. The man too seemed to be the worse for wear. Not the kind of man you'd ever pay attention to if you saw him in a conventional lunchtime crowd, but here, among the sleek and the beautiful, he stood out. Roxy wondered who he was. A gate crasher, she thought, with some amusement. A retiree from someplace like Washington Heights who had nothing better to do with his days than to find out where the action was and to insinuate himself into it. Everybody wanted a piece of Jonathan.

"Marvelous job, Jonathan," said fashion photographer Helmut Briggs, who would be shooting a fashion spread for *Vogue* at the hotel later in the week. "I can't wait to work here."

It was almost time for her to go back to work. She stood there for another moment, waiting to catch Jonathan's eye, to wave goodbye. The next moment was dreamlike, as she saw the gray man, the gate crasher, take a revolver from his pocket, his expression unchanged.

"Jonathan!" she screamed.

As he turned to her, there was a shot. He fell. Another shot and someone else fell. There was blood on the steps. People ran after the gray man. There was screaming. She was screaming.

"Make room! Make room!" someone yelled. Roxy stood still; she couldn't move. Stella was forcing her way through the circle that had formed around Jonathan's fallen figure. "He's my husband!" Stella was screaming. "He's my husband!" And she clawed her way through and kneeled down beside Jonathan and she got blood on her suit and she cradled his head. There were ambulance sirens and Roxy staggered up the steps to where Jonathan lay stricken, but the crowd was too tight—she couldn't push her way through—and Stella was protecting him and wouldn't let anyone get close. Jonathan, Roxy thought, as she stood there frozen, unable to wake up from the dream.

IT HAD BEEN a long time since Roxy Monahan had had a rosary in her hands, but she held one now, as she sat in the waiting room on the fifth floor of New York Hospital. Jonathan was in emergency surgery and his chances were not good.

"He'll be all right, Roxy," said her brother Joseph, who had brought the rosary. He was the only one of her brothers to have left the sailor's life behind in order to dedicate himself to his religion.

"I don't know, Joe," she said. "I can't help but have the feeling that as soon as some happiness comes into my life I lose it all."

"You are committing the sin of vanity, Roxy," said Joseph. "The Lord is not lying in wait to punish *you*, no matter what you may think you've done."

His tone was not by any means condemnatory. He was a loving person who had rushed to be with her, and she realized now that she had been missing him badly. When he'd become a priest, she'd begun to think of him less as a brother. Now, as they sat side by side, she told herself that she must never lose him again.

"It hasn't been easy for me to trust, Joseph, to fall in love. We're a defensive bunch, aren't we?" she said ruefully. "The world against the Monahans. And now, just as I've managed to break down those defenses, this happens . . ." She looked away. Tears formed in her eyes, but she had to hold herself together. She had to be there with all the clarity and purpose she could muster. There was time yet to cry.

"Pray, Roxy. Put yourself in the Lord's hands. Jesus loves you."

She nodded, and followed him in the words of the catechism. As she did so, the horrible spectacle kept replaying. The gun, the blood, the elderly man wrestled to the ground. But why? And when she saw the gun, why hadn't she flown to Jonathan's side, to protect him, to keep him from being where he was now?

As she sat there, first with her brother Joe and later with her father and her other brothers, she was joined by Sidney Farrell and Lotte. Both of them were gray-faced, anguished. Sidney kept shaking his head. "I can't believe this," he said. "This is a dream. I'm going to wake up from this."

"It's not a dream," said Lotte, chain-smoking Parliaments. "The name for it is lousy, stinking real life. The good ones get shot. The bad ones retire."

"Well, who is this, this fiend who shot him?" Sidney demanded. "Has anyone gotten any hard facts?"

Roxy closed her eyes. She was bone-tired, and this endless night stretched ahead of her. "We haven't even gotten any soft facts yet," she said. "But we will."

In another few hours Merry Broad was located and

she arrived from Connecticut where she had gone for a few days. She and Roxy looked at each other for a long moment, and then excused themselves to a private room.

"You're the woman my brother's been seeing?" Merry asked bluntly.

"Yes," said Roxy. "I was there when he was shot."

"I see," said Merry.

Roxy had little patience for people who said "I see" when they saw nothing. She knew that she and Jonathan were close, but Merry seemed aloof and brittle and suspicious.

"And you've had no word on his condition yet?" asked Merry.

"He's still in surgery. He's been there for eight hours." For a moment she couldn't speak. "I don't want to think what it would take eight hours to fix."

Merry nodded stiffly. "I appreciate your being here, Miss Monahan. Of course, if you wish to go home now and get some badly needed rest, please do so. I will be speaking with the doctors from now on."

The way it had since she was a carrot-topped little girl, her face turned a bright strawberry red. She wasn't prepared for this, and she felt her adrenalin start to pump through her. "I don't intend to go anywhere, Miss Broad," she said. "I intend to stay right here and I intend to ask the doctors my own questions."

"I see," said Merry.

"What do you *see*," demanded Roxy, her Irish up. "I see a woman being unnecessarily and inappropriately rude to another woman. And I don't get it."

"I don't know you, Miss Monahan," said Merry.

"And I have no reason to trust the women my brother becomes involved with."

"Listen," Roxy said. "I don't want to get off on the wrong foot here. I love your brother and he loves me. And I know you love him. I think two people who love the same person should try to work together, don't you?"

Merry stared at her, her eyes still filled with mistrust.

"I know the sort of woman your brother was married to, *is* married to," she amended. "But I'm not that sort. Now you can decide whether you want to hate me and be suspicious, or you can decide that you want to trust me. I suggest you do the latter, but either way I'm not going to disappear."

Merry was silent for another long moment, then nodded. "Very well then. Let's go find ourselves a doctor, shall we?" she suggested.

But the doctor found them. There was that moment —that unbearable moment—when the roll of the dice was about to be revealed. "The operation appears to have been successful," said the doctor, a tall man in his mid-thirties, with expressive eyes and a droopy moustache. "There was considerable internal bleeding, but the bullet avoided the major organs and arteries, and Mr. Broad is expected to survive, barring any unusual postoperative problems."

Merry suddenly sagged, with relief or fatigue or some combination therof. Roxy reached out to support her, and, at first, Merry tensed from her touch, but then she relaxed. They returned to the others to tell them the news. Lotte, generally about as emotional as a clam, burst into tears. The Monahan brothers

263

cheered. Sidney went off to meet with the reporters. Merry and Roxy sat together. "Why did that man do it?" Merry demanded. "Why was my brother shot?"

"The police have the assailant," said Roxy. "I have every confidence they'll get to the bottom of this."

"I'm going to go down to police headquarters immediately," said Merry. "I want to know what really happened, why it happened, and what's being done!"

"You've just arrived," said Roxy. "Why don't you rest up a bit? You'll be no good by tomorrow."

Merry stood up. "Thanks. I appreciate your concern, but I'm going down there."

As Roxy walked her to the elevator, they discussed plans for tomorrow. Between the two of them, they would keep a constant vigil. "You can't trust nursing care anywhere," said Merry. "Only those who really care," she said significantly, looking into Roxy's eyes, "can be counted on."

And then the elevator door opened and out walked Stella. She was an imposing figure in her lynx coat, her high black leather boots, her mane of hair—the grieving soon-to-be widow, her face a study in anguish. "Where's Jonathan?" she demanded.

"What are you doing here?" Merry returned.

There were mascara stains on Stella's cheek, showing she had wept. "I don't have to justify myself to you," she said. "Where is he?"

"That's none of your concern," said Merry, stronger now, ready to do battle.

"I demand to see him!"

"I'd as soon permit you to see him as I would Typhoid Mary," Merry replied scathingly.

"If you don't, I'll make a scene . . ."

"You already have,"said Merry. "Now why don't you just leave like a good little girl, Stella? Your act is getting tiresome."

Stella began to walk on and Merry jumped in front of her, blocking her way.

"Mrs. Broad," Roxy said, "please!"

Stella turned to fix her with a deadly stare. "To whom are you speaking?" she said. "I have more claim to be here than his latest chippie does."

"You have no claims on anyone," said Merry. "I want you out. I know some dirty secrets about you and I'll spread them far and wide if I have to. I love my brother and I won't stand to see him . . ."

"You don't love him," Stella interrupted, her tone growing guttural and coarse. "You're *in* love with him. It's Jonathan, only Jonathan, who gets your little motor . . ."

With all her might, Merry slapped her across the face. Stella gave out an involuntary cry and reached up to touch her flaming cheek. "You saw what she did," she cried to Roxy. "I'll slap her with a lawsuit that will make her wish she never . . ."

"See you in court, Stella," Merry shot back. "Now move it."

Stella began to say something else, but she stopped herself and turned toward the elevator. Just before she got on, she reconsidered and turned to a shocked nurse who had witnessed the entire proceedings. "Tell Mr. Broad his wife was here to see him," she said with all her dignity, and she boarded the elevator and was gone.

All through the next day, Merry and Roxy waited by Jonathan's bedside. Roxy sat there going over some briefs with a red pencil. Merry had a stack of French magazines, from which she was clipping articles. Every now and then, one or the other of them would go downstairs and come back with some fresh coffee or bouillon or peanuts. By the end of the day, they felt that they had known each other all their lives and unexpectedly they felt the beginnings of a friendship.

At 9:25 P.M. the day after the attempt on his life, Jonathan Broad stirred with a groan. Merry and Roxy rushed to his side. The groaning intensified and then, slowly, he opened his eyes.

"Jonathan, can you hear me?" Merry cried.

He stared at the two women, bringing them into focus, nodding slowly, heavily.

"Are you all right, Jonathan?" Roxy asked tearfully.

"I . . . where . . ."

"You're back, Jonathan," Roxy said. "A terrible thing happened to you, but you're back. And we're here for you, Jonathan. We'll always be here, always."

He moved slightly and then winced. "Oh, God," he said. "It hurts."

"Do you remember anything, Jonathan?" Merry asked.

He shook his head. "I was at the hotel. I was shaking hands. Then there was a . . . was there an explosion?"

The two women looked at each other. There had been an explosion of a sort, Roxy thought. A highly focused explosion, that ripped its way through Jonathan's ribcage. "You were shot, Jonathan," said Merry. "Someone tried to kill you."

"What are you saying?" Jonathan replied. "I don't understand."

"You were shot." Merry repeated. "You almost died. But you've pulled through."

"Who was it?"

"A man named Maximilian Weber," Roxy replied. "Have you ever heard that name?"

He shook his head. "Did he say . . . did he give a reason?"

"He told the police that he was a tenant in a building owned by the Broad Company, a building in Bay Ridge. He's a retired butcher, seventy-one years old, and has a wife who's dying of cancer. It seems that the managing agent has been withholding services in response to Weber's not paying his rent bill. An eviction process had been instituted."

There was a silence. "But that's terrible." The Broad Company would never . . ." He was too weak to finish his thought.

"Jonathan, please," said Roxy, "you've got to rest. The important thing is that you're back, darling, and you're here to stay." But even before she'd gotten all her words out, Roxy saw that he was asleep. She touched his wan cheek and thanked God for what He had given back to her.

"I see," said Stella. "Thank you," she added, hanging up the receiver. She turned to Gabriel, who was sitting up in bed. watching a rerun of "The Rockford Files." "He's in fair condition."

"Huh?"

"I said he's in fair condition. Stable. Surviving," she said, spitting the words out.

"Goddamn it."

"Point blank range," she fumed. "And he blew it."

"It's that girlfriend of his. Called out to him at the

last moment and Broad lurched forward. That's what the TV news said, anyway."

"It's not his girlfriend, it's the gun you hired," she said furiously. "Some old fart. I could have done better than he did."

"I bet you could," he said. "Now shut up. I'm watching this show."

"You're watching this show?" she said incredulously. "Our whole game plan just went down the toilet and you're watching this show?"

"Stifle it, babe. It's too late."

"Not only are we left holding the bag, but the cops have a songbird who's going to save his hide." As he watched his show she felt her blood boil. She hated him; she hated every man she'd ever known. On an impulse, she reached over and turned off the television and turned around to face him, her eyes blazing.

"Put it back on," he said.

"Listen, you don't seem very connected," she said. "You don't seem to understand that you sent a guy out to do a job and he screwed it up just about as royally as someone could possibly . . ." But she didn't get the last words out. Like an attack dog, he was on her, whipping her around the face and the breasts and the arms with the flat of his open hand.

"Stop it!" she shrieked. "Stop it! You're hurting me!"

"Goddamn bitch!" he muttered. "Pulling me into your stupid goddamn schemes. You're nothing but trouble."

"Stop! Gabe! Stop!"

He stopped. He backed away from her, breathing hard. She tried to think quickly. "Now listen," she said. "This is crazy. If we fight with each other, we'll absolutely blow this whole thing. We can still remedy this," she said, trying to convince him, to convince herself. In her anger and disappointment, she had momentarily forgotten how dangerous he was. She shouldn't ever forget. "We'll come out of this, Gabe. Don't worry."

He looked at her, his eyes dead and scary, and then turned back to "The Rockford Files." She went into the bathroom and put cold water on her bruises.

DISGRUNTLED TENANT FELLS
EMPIRE BUILDER

EVICTION PROCESS RESULTS IN
ASSASSINATION ATTEMPT

"I HAD NOTHING LEFT TO LOSE,"
CLAIMS OUSTED TENANT

The headlines on the tabloids assaulted Jonathan and, in a rage, he threw them across the room.

"Don't upset yourself," said Lotte, who was sitting by his bedside taking dictation. Jonathan felt that the only way to really keep his head together was to get back to work as soon as possible, and so Lotte had punched the clock this morning at seven, as usual.

"What do you mean? 'Don't upset yourself,'" he demanded.

She thought a moment. "Got me," she said with a shrug. "I figured I'd give it a try."

He made himself get out of bed. Despite the length of operating time, most of which had to do with stemming internal bleeding, his injuries were not of the sort to prevent a speedy recovery. He was ex-

270

pected to be on his feet already, to walk around, to recapture his strength. Six days of sitting in a hospital bed was an immobility he had never before experienced, and he could unequivocally state that it made him crazy.

"You're doing just fine," Lotte said. "Look at you. Another few days and you'll go home."

There was a silence. He didn't seem to be expressing the kind of enthusiasm about leaving that she expected from him. "What's the matter?" she said.

"Nothing."

"What 'nothing'? I know you better than that. Tell Lotte."

He sat down on one of the chairs in the room and held his side. "This place is safe," he said.

"What are you talking about?" she said, genuinely confused.

"It's a miracle I'm here to tell the tale, Lotte," he said. "Maybe that was only a first try."

"Oh, stop it," she scolded. "You're being morbid. This was one of your grade-A variety New York City nuts. You happened to be in the wrong place when the nut fell from the tree."

He shook his head. "I don't think so, Lotte. Maybe it's crazy, but I feel like someone's looking at me down the barrel of a gun."

"You're just shellshocked, sweetie," she said. "You need a rest. Would it be insane of me to suggest that you go on a holiday? I know such a thing has never been considered before . . ."

"Right," he snapped. "I'm going to go on a vacation. Let my projects collapse. See River Park go down the tubes."

"Nothing will collapse. Nothing will go down the

271

tubes," she said firmly. "Sidney and I will keep the home fires burning. And you could spend a few weeks going through the French countryside on a canal boat or something pleasant like that."

"Forget it."

"With someone very nice to nurse you back to health. Like Roxy. A *special* trip that two people make after a *special* ceremony, hint, hint."

"Lotte, please . . ."

"Forget River Park for a minute, will you? Forget everything but this terrific gal you should be spending the rest of your life with."

Lotte's words stayed in his mind. When Roxy came to visit after work, she became aware of his staring at her in this extraordinarily intense way. "What's the matter?"

He decided to put it bluntly; such was his way. "When I get out of here, I want to live with you. Do you want to live with me?"

A shy little smile came to her lips. "Of course I want to live with you."

He nodded briskly, and then, a moment later, he smiled. "When do you want to move in?"

"Excuse me?" she said. "I think you've got it backwards."

He looked at her, confused. "What do you mean?"

"I'm not moving into your 'palace,' Jonathan, your acre in the sky. I told you a while back, that I'm a Red Hook girl, born and bred. If you want me, that's part of the deal."

She had to be kidding, right? He had what was probably the most spectacular private residence in the most spectacular city in the world. "Come on, Roxy. I can't very well move out of my own building. Think about it. People will think something's terribly wrong with the Palace. They'll think there's dry rot or toxic waste or that the American roach is moving up from the basement."

"There *is* something terribly wrong with the Palace," she said. "It has nothing to do with me. I don't want moats and Jacuzzis and saunas and video rooms. I want you, but I don't want the trappings."

Just then there was a knock at the door. "Mr. Broad, may I come in?" asked a police detective.

It was Detective Briggs, with whom Jonathan had spoken several times before.

"Yes, Detective, please. Come in."

The small-framed, dapper man nodded to Roxy and took a seat by Jonathan's bed. "We have a break in the case, Mr. Broad," Briggs reported.

Jonathan and Roxy shared a look. "What's that, Detective?" Jonathan asked.

"The FBI have run prints on Maximilian Weber. His real name is Gunther Herrmann. He entered this country in 1948, under the name Max Pietroff. Gunther Herrmann is a wanted Nazi war criminal. He was brought into this country through an Italian connection, and we have reason to believe that he has operated as a hired killer for organized crime."

The silence that followed was palpable, broken when Detective Briggs continued. "Mr. Broad," he said, "let me ask you bluntly. Have you had any dealings with organized crime figures?"

"No, sir, I have not," Jonathan said. "But," he added, after a moment, "my wife has."

* * *

It was shortly before eight o'clock in the evening when Gabriel Messina received a call from a police officer who was a friend of the family. "They've traced Weber," the cop said from a phone booth. "The clock is ticking, Gabriel."

Within the hour, a plane was waiting to take him and Stella to Miami. Stella had never liked Miami— certainly not these days, when it wasn't much more than little Cuba and had nothing going for it beyond Don Johnson—but she had no other choice than to go. Once there, she'd regroup, figure out what to do next.

As the plane took off, Gabriel poured them each a Jack Daniels. As she sipped the sweet-hot liquor, she felt gratified that she had won him over once again. But then it wasn't hard, she thought, winning over men.

"Comfy?" he asked her.

"Yes," she replied, with a smile she tried to keep from being tentative.

"Cheese? Crackers?" he offered.

"No. I never eat when I fly."

A few moments after they were airborne he was snoring. His mouth was open and gummy-looking and she stared at him in disgust. She hated men. Jonathan, Gabriel, Wayne Mullins, Anderson Kendall —she hated them all. She hated her father for deserting her before she'd even known him. She hated her stepfather for making her do the dirty things. She hated all the men who had used her and given her things and took things away from her.

She closed her eyes and looked down on the city, with its sparkling lights, lights that she had once owned. She loved this city, she thought, with an odd wistfulness, and wondered how long it would be before she could return.

It was almost eleven o'clock when Jonathan's door opened. Half-asleep, Jonathan became aware of a presence in his room. The first thought that came into his mind was that it was someone come back to finish off the job.

"Jonathan?" a voice whispered in the dark.

"Who is it?"

"Anderson. Please, Jonathan. I have to talk to you."

When Jonathan turned on the light, he saw the usually impeccable Anderson looking disheveled, almost seedy. "How did you get in here?" Jonathan demanded. "I'm going to ring the nurse . . ."

"No, Jonathan. Please," Anderson implored. "I sneaked in here. I had to see you. Just give me a few moments."

Jonathan stared at him. "What do you want?"

"Ever since I heard what happened to you, I've felt compelled to talk to you. I never believed the story about Weber . . ."

"Get to the point," Jonathan said.

"Stella wanted me to join her in a company, a front for Gabriel Messina. I went along with it—gladly. But it wasn't so much because I was out to get you. Sure, I wanted what you had. But that wasn't all. I was deep in a hole, Jonathan. Gambling, drugs—I was out of control. You never knew it. Very few people knew it. I've always been first-rate at putting on a front."

"You sure have," said Jonathan. "And this is all very moving, but I've heard enough . . ."

"I didn't come here tonight thinking you'd take pity on me," Anderson said, with a last vestige of self-respect. "I came here to tell you that it's my belief that Max Weber was hired by Gabriel Messina and by . . . by Stella to kill you."

Jonathan gave the shattered young man a hard look. "Will you tell what you just told me to the police?" he asked.

Anderson thought a moment, chewing his lower lip. "I have no other choice now, do I, Jonathan? Even though it means that when I get through with this I'll be a dead man."

There was a long moment of silence. "I'll see to it, as best as I can, that you're protected, Anderson. But, no, you have no other choice."

The weather south of Miami was incredibly muggy. Any minute now, Stella thought, it would rain, one of those tropical downpours that would thrash the palms around and get under your skin and leave everything smelling of mildew. She remembered now just how much she hated Florida, its coconuts and tourists and old people. She hated being here and she hated having to run.

They were driving down to the Keys and from there they would take a boat to Eleuthera. But the trip was a killer. All she could get on the radio was country and western. "Shit," she said. "Every time you go south, you have to listen to this hillbilly crap."

"Plug in a cassette," he said.

"The selection's no better," she complained. The rain was starting to fall, big noisy drops, that had the same blunt sound as winged insects splattering against the windshield.

"What's the matter? You haven't done anything but bitch since we got here," Gabriel said.

"I don't like Florida, all right?"

"You like the Tombs better, baby?"

She pulled out a cigarette and lit it up, filling the car with cigarette smoke.

After a while, they stopped at a greasy spoon on the road. She had tea and a disgusting sweet bun; he ate whatever tomato slop was masquerading on the menu as Italian. She went to buy the *Miami Herald* and buried herself in it so she didn't have to look at the tomato specks in the corners of his mouth.

The Weber story was all over the paper. They were getting out just in time. She had to give Gabriel that much—he knew when to run. Thank God, he'd taken her with him. Imagine what it would be like in jail, with all the bull-dykes wanting to punish her just because she'd once had money and a place in the palace. Imagine what it would be like to go on trial, to have Jonathan staring at her with his dumb cow eyes, to have her lawyer making a bundle and throwing in the towel anyway. "Let's go," she said, getting nervous. "It's time."

"Wait a minute, will ya?" he said, sucking in a strand of spaghetti.

"Jesus, how can you eat that slop?" she said contemptuously.

The road became less traveled, wilder. Mangrove trees were everywhere, and gulls, and some kind of big black bird that gave her the creeps. She thought about the snakes in the mangroves and felt cold even though the temperature was ninety-three. The radio was blaring a country song—"I Never Loved or Lived Until I Loved You"—and Gabriel kept belching and farting.

"Can't you control it?" she said finally.

"No, I can't. OK?"

He pulled onto a small dirt road parallel to the main road. "Now what are you doing?" she asked.

"I gotta take a dump."

"Couldn't you do it back in the restaurant?"

"Hey. Cool out, OK?"

The dirt road got rockier and more overgrown with rank waist-high weeds. He parked the car and got out. She sat there, feeling sick to her stomach. Why was he taking such a long time? Maybe he'd been bitten by a snake, she thought, with a childish sense of glee. Maybe one of those pretty little coral snakes slithered right up to his heinie and took a bite. She smoked another cigarette and thought about what she would do when she got to Eleuthera. Contact Anderson. At least he could get some money to her; that's the least he could do. And what about Wayne? Maybe she could stoke two fires. The thing was, she realized as she smoked the cigarette down to the filter, she was feeling kind of low. Low was running, and sitting by the side of the road and waiting while a man you hated finished up his business. "Stella!" he called. "You got some tissue?"

Oh Jesus. Could you believe it? She looked in the glove compartment and found a box. "Yeah," she said, irritated. She was badly affected by the heat. "There's some here."

"Well, bring it over."

"No way. Come and get it."

"Bring it to me now!" he shouted.

She sighed bitterly and got out of the car, pushing her way through some horrible, leathery fronds until she came into a sort of clearing and there he was. "Thanks," he said, aiming the semi-automatic at her.

"No," she said. What a fool she was. "No . . .", but she didn't finish. The bullets tore into her, tossing her around like a rag doll. She wound up at the base of a tree covered with thick coiled vines, a thread of life in her yet. "No," she breathed, watching him come to her. He put the barrel of the gun against her eye and fired.

He didn't want to be wheeled out of the hospital.

"But it's hospital regulations, Mr. Broad!" a nurse cried.

He was not going to exit the hospital, into the crowd of reporters and photographers, in a wheelchair, looking like a beaten man. "Arrest me," he said, getting up, supporting himself on the arm of his trainer Pablo, who would be helping him home today and working with him in the oncoming weeks to help him regain his strength.

"They're ready for you, Jonathan," said Roxy, with tears in her eyes, as she watched him struggle to walk. Death had come so close, touching their lives, but they had chased it away.

"I'm ready," he said.

As he emerged from the hospital, the flashbulbs popped, and he smiled and waved and thanked everyone for coming out to see him.

"What are your immediate plans, Jonathan?" called Fred Wayne of NBC.

"My immediate plan is to not go skiing for a while," he joked. "My longer range plan is to see River Park through."

"What are the odds of that?" asked Lola Curtin of *Time*.

"I'm not worrying about the odds, Lola," said

279

Jonathan. "If I believed in odds, I wouldn't be here right now. Let's just say I plan to go about business as usual."

"Do you expect your wife's disappearance and rumors of her connections to organized crime to set you back?" asked a young woman from *USA Today*.

He looked around the circle. "It's not going to be easy," he declared, "but I'm going to do the best I can. I believe in New York City and I believe in River Park. Above all, I believe in what River Park could mean to the future of this city. Thank you, ladies and gentlemen."

He and Roxy and Pablo got into the car, and Fergus headed up the FDR Drive. "You were good out there, bud," Roxy said. "*I* believed you, anyway."

He looked at her and then looked out the window. "It's damned good to be alive," he said, his voice thick with emotion.

"Given the alternatives," she replied jokingly, trying to cover up her own emotion.

"I'm not thinking about any alternatives," he said. "I know what I want and I'm going to get it."

"A man of action." she cracked. 'Go after what you want and bag it."

"You're going to marry me, Madame Deputy Commissioner," he said. "Very soon. As soon as we can walk down the aisle together, just you and me, without Pablo. No offense, Pablo," he said.

"None taken, señor," the abashed Pablo replied.

She laughed. "You think you can have your way entirely, huh?"

"Yep."

"I'm *not* moving into the Palace," she reminded him.

"I know that."

"I'm keeping my loft."

"Listen, I've got it all figured out," he said. "We compromise. Halfway between the Palace and your loft is West 11th Street. We buy a town house with a garden big enough for a playset for the kids and . . ."

"Oh, Jonathan."

". . . and we keep the loft as a vacation home. Put in a pool, sauna, skating rink . . ."

"The crazy thing is I think you're half serious," she charged.

He stared at her, a gleam in his eye, and didn't deny it.

"I don't know, Jonathan," she said, shaking her head. "It's not what I expected."

"Life is full of surprises, babe," he said, as he took her into his arms and swore that he would never let her go.

KARL F. FURST

THE WHITE KNIGHT

Lucas Paulson had always been the driving force behind the HEST Corporation. The original idea had come out of the group of them in those laid-back California campus days – and nights – when minds – and bodies – had met, tangled and explored. The hard science expertise: that came from the others. But Paulson had been the one who had seen just how ideas could be turned into hi-tech reality. Who'd hustled to raise the capital, hustled to sell the product, hustled to build the company from local to national, to international account.

And now everything was under threat. Now he had to fight with that same guts and cunning and luck to hold what he'd created.

POST A LITTLE HAPPINESS

Post·A·Book

A Royal Mail service in association with the Book Marketing Council & The Booksellers Association.

Post-A-Book is a Post Office trademark.

MORE FICTION FROM
HODDER AND STOUGHTON PAPERBACKS